LIFE SKILLS

Preparing Students for the Future

BY

MYRL SHIREMAN

COPYRIGHT © 2009 Mark Twain Media, Inc.

ISBN 978-1-58037-512-2

Printing No. CD-404115

Mark Twain Media, Inc., Publishers
Distributed by Carson-Dellosa Publishing Company, Inc.

Visit us at www.carsondellosa.com

TABLE OF CONTENTS

TABLE OF CONTENTS (cont.)

INTRODUCTION

Society today has the challenge of encouraging young people to live a healthy lifestyle. A healthy lifestyle, not just for today, but for continued success in tomorrow's world, includes making good choices about the foods we eat and the amount of exercise we get. However, a healthy lifestyle is about much more than food and exercise. A healthy lifestyle for today's young people includes developing decision-making skills that relate to social relationships. A healthy lifestyle includes being aware of the dangers of such things as sexually transmitted diseases, drug and alcohol abuse, and smoking. Students must also understand the perils of environmental risks such as spending too much unprotected time in the sunlight. Additionally, if young people are going to be able to maintain a healthy lifestyle, they must make decisions about financial matters.

In helping young people develop healthy lifestyle habits, adults must be able to listen to the concerns of young people and find out what they are thinking. Who and what are the influencing factors in their lives? What significant information do they not have about critical lifestyle issues? Why do they not practice a healthy lifestyle? What are their biases and prejudices? Helping young people develop habits that lead to a healthy lifestyle requires that adults must understand there are no short cuts to getting young people to accept and practice a healthy lifestyle. A critical first step is to make sure that young people have the information that will encourage them to lead a healthy lifestyle.

This book includes many activities that provide factual information about healthy lifestyle issues. Most of the activities may be used to stimulate student responses and foster class discussion. The student responses and discussion provide the classroom teacher with insights to positively guide students in making healthy lifestyle decisions.

The National Science Education Standards state that students should develop an understanding of personal health. The standards emphasize the importance of students understanding that exercise is key to the maintenance and improvement of health, that the use of tobacco increases the risk of illness, and that alcohol and drugs are often abused. Students should understand how critical food is for energy and nutrients during growth and development. Students must know that sexual activity is a means of transmitting disease. Additionally, students must be aware of the risks in the environment that are detrimental to a healthy lifestyle.

Name: _____ Date: _____

ANTIOXIDANTS

Antioxidants are nutrients in the food we eat. Antioxidants can slow or prevent damage to cells caused by free radicals. Free radicals are atoms missing an electron. They cause damage to a body's cells by stealing electrons away. Antioxidants act like guards that keep free radicals from stealing your electrons. It is also believed that antioxidants may prevent some forms of cancer. Vitamin A, vitamin C, vitamin E, and selenium are antioxidants.

Antioxidants are also found in beans, grains, fruits, and vegetables. Fruits and vegetables contain flavonoids, lycopene, lutein, lignan, and carotenoids, which are all antioxidants. However, each of these antioxidants are more common in some foods than others. Flavonoids are found in blueberries, purple grapes, apples, cranberries, strawberries, tea, dark chocolate, grape juice, red berries, soybeans, and raspberries. Lycopene is found in red tomatoes. Foods like brussels sprouts, spinach, and broccoli contain lutein. Flax seed is a food rich in lignan. Carrots are rich in beta-carotene, which is a carotenoid.

Antioxidants have been proven to be important to one's health. How can we get more antioxidants? The best way is to have five or more servings of fruits and vegetables each day. Eating fruits and vegetables from different color groups is very important. This is because different colored fruits and vegetables are rich sources of different kinds of antioxidants.

1. Under each color, write at least one vegetable that you like.

Red	Blue	Yellow	Orange	Green
_____	_____	_____	_____	_____
_____	_____	_____	_____	_____
_____	_____	_____	_____	_____

2. Under each color, write at least one fruit that you like.

Red	Blue	Yellow	Orange	Green
_____	_____	_____	_____	_____
_____	_____	_____	_____	_____
_____	_____	_____	_____	_____

3. Listed below are antioxidants found in fruits and vegetables. Place the letter for the antioxidant on the blank beside each food that contains that antioxidant.

A. Flavonoid   B. Lycopene   C. Lutein   D. Carotenoid   E. Lignan

____ blueberries   ____ red tomatoes   ____ purple grapes   ____ apples

____ cranberries   ____ strawberries   ____ tea   ____ soybeans

____ brussels sprouts   ____ grape juice   ____ red berries   ____ spinach

____ dark chocolate   ____ raspberries   ____ broccoli   ____ flax seeds

____ carrots

Name: _____ Date: _____

FATS

Fat is an important part of a healthy lifestyle diet. However, it is necessary to limit the total amount of fat and the kind of fat in our diet. The American Heart Association recommends keeping <u>total fat</u> consumption to less than 35% of daily calories. Fats include saturated fats, unsaturated fats, monounsaturated fats, polyunsaturated fats, and trans fats.

Saturated Fats

Saturated fats are fats found in foods made from animal products. These fats are solid at room temperature. Saturated fats must be limited because they may clog the arteries. Clogged arteries lead to heart problems and possibly strokes. Saturated fats are found in meat, butter, cheese, palm oil, ice cream, hot dogs, and whole milk. Saturated fats should be limited to 12 to 16 grams of the daily diet.

Monounsaturated and Polyunsaturated Fats

Monounsaturated and polyunsaturated are both unsaturated fats. Unsaturated fats are liquid at room temperature. Unsaturated fats come from plant sources.

Monounsaturated Fats

Monounsaturated fats are found in canola oil, soybean oil, and olive oil. This fat is very healthy. Foods with monounsaturated fats are beneficial because monounsaturated fat improves the levels of HDL (good) cholesterol and lowers the levels of LDL (bad) cholesterol.

Polyunsaturated Fats

Some reports show that polyunsaturated fats lower LDL (bad) cholesterol. These fats are found in corn oil, sunflower oil, and soybean oil and in some nuts like walnuts. Fish like salmon and herring are also sources of polyunsaturated fats.

Trans Fats

Trans fats are found in many baked goods. These fats are formed when vegetable oils are hydrogenated to extend shelf life. Hydrogenated means hydrogen is added to plant oil by heating the oil. The problem is, fat made in this manner raises LDL cholesterol and lowers HDL cholesterol. Trans fats should be avoided in the foods you consume. Read food labels carefully because cookies, cakes, crackers, bread, and chips may have trans fats, which may also be called partially hydrogenated oils. Look for foods with 0% trans fats.

Omega-3 Fatty Acids

Omega-3 fatty acids are found in some fish. Salmon, trout, halibut, herring, and sardines are fish high in Omega-3 fatty acids. Everyone should try to eat fish two to three times per week. Omega-3 has many benefits for those who lead a healthy lifestyle. Omega-3 fatty acids tend to lessen the likelihood of heart attack and stroke. Omega-3 fatty acids are also found in plants like walnuts, flax seed, and foods made from soybeans.

Name: _____ Date: _____

FINDING THE NUMBER OF CALORIES FROM FAT

In our daily diet, the total amount of fat should be limited to 35% of our daily calories. The amount of saturated fat should be limited to 7% of our daily total fat intake.

Remember, 35% changed to a decimal is 0.35. To change 7% to a decimal, the decimal point must be moved two places to the left, which is then written as 0.07.

Find the total fat calories for each of the following daily diets. Multiply each of the following calorie amounts by 0.35 to find the number of total fat calories you should not go over. Then multiply the answer by 0.07 to find the number of saturated fat calories you should not go over.

Example: 1,800-calorie diet

1,800 x 0.35 = 630   Total fat calories per day

630 x 0.07 = 44.1   Saturated fat calories per day

1,600-calorie diet

1.   1,600 x 0.35 = _____   Total fat calories per day

2.   _____ x 0.07 = _____   Saturated fat calories per day

2,000-calorie diet

3.   2,000 x 0.35 = _____   Total fat calories per day

4.   _____ x 0.07 = _____   Saturated fat calories per day

2,500-calorie diet

5.   2,500 x 0.35 = _____   Total fat calories per day

6.   _____ x 0.07 = _____   Saturated fat calories per day

Name: _____ Date: _____

FAT CLOZE EXERCISE

Read the cloze paragraph below. Complete the blanks using the words listed.

**herring   omega-3   walnuts   fat   salmon   cholesterol
polyunsaturated   plant   saturated   limited**

A healthy lifestyle diet includes a measured amount of fat. It is important to balance the fat in one's diet between saturated fats, monounsaturated fats, and polyunsaturated fats. A diet for a healthy lifestyle may include calories from all three of these **1)** _____ sources. The fat from red meat and dairy products is **2)** _____ fat. These fats are solid at room temperature. Because the fats from these sources are likely to increase the **3)** _____ level, a healthy lifestyle diet limits saturated fat to seven percent of the required daily fat intake. Therefore, the amount of fat from these sources should be **4)** _____. A diet for a healthy lifestyle includes an increase in the fat from monounsaturated and **5)** _____ fat sources. Fat from these sources include the **6)** _____ oils like olive oil, canola oil, sunflower seeds, soybeans, and peanuts. The fat from eating certain kinds of fish has been found to be very beneficial. Many fish contain **7)** _____ fatty acid, which is very good for the heart. Two fish that are good sources of omega-3 fats are **8)** _____ and **9)** _____. A healthy lifestyle diet should include fish on a weekly basis. A nut that is rich in plant omega-3 is **10)** _____.

hydrogenated   limited   hydrogen   fat   cholesterol   shortening

The amount of calories from fat in the diet should be limited to approximately one-third of the daily diet. Additionally, no more than seven percent of the fat intake should be from saturated **11)** _____ sources. When unsaturated fats are processed and **12)** _____ is added, the fat becomes solid at room temperature. The change results in hydrogenated or partially hydrogenated fats, also called trans fats. Hydrogenated fats increase **13)** _____ levels, so they must be used sparingly. When selecting foods, it is important to check the food label for the amount of **14)** _____ fat. Hydrogenated fats are most often found in foods like **15)** _____ and baked goods. Therefore, foods with hydrogenated fat such as shortenings and baked goods should be **16)** _____ in the healthy lifestyle diet.

Name: _____ Date: _____

 # SOURCES OF FAT: GRAPHIC ORGANIZER

Complete the following graphic organizer for fats. In the blanks under the headings for **saturated, monounsaturated, polyunsaturated,** and **trans fat,** place the following sources of each type of fat.

butter	**canola oil**	**cookies**	**palm oil**	**hot dogs**
soybean oil	**whole milk**	**cakes**	**crackers**	**sunflower seeds**
bread	**cheese**	**chips**	**olive oil**	**corn**

Saturated

_____

_____

_____

_____

_____

Trans Fat

_____

_____

_____

_____

_____

Types of Fat

Monounsaturated

_____

_____

Polyunsaturated

_____

_____

_____

Name: _____ Date: _____

REVIEWING FAT: GRAPHIC ORGANIZER

A diet including too much fat is unhealthy. In this exercise, fill in the rectangles with the words and phrases listed below.

unsaturated fat | most vegetable oils | saturated fats
heart disease | liquid at room temperature | fats
problems with too much | solid at room temperature | stroke
fatty buildup in arteries | animal fat/some vegetable oils

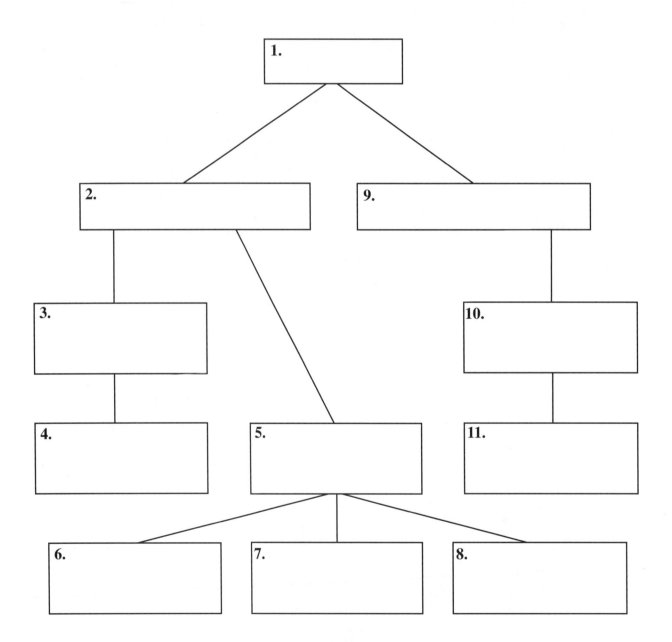

Name: _____ Date: _____

 # WEIGHTY MATTERS

In the food pyramid on page 24, note it suggests that you eat sparingly of foods high in fat content. It is suggested that no more than 35 percent of the calories that you consume in a day come from fat. In the following chart, some foods are listed from the four major food groups. The number of calories, grams of fat, grams of protein, and grams of carbohydrates are listed for each item.

Food	Calories	Fat (g)	Protein (g)	Carbohydrates (g)
hamburger	560	29	31	34
hot dog	280	17	11	2
spaghetti	250	9	8	37
banana	80	0	1	21
apple	80	1	0.4	20
cookie	50	3	1	6
1 piece fried chicken	140	8	14	2
grapefruit	56	0	0.5	12
taco	190	8	15	15
teaspoon butter	100	12	0	0
pizza	450	15	25	55
12 french fries	210	11	3	25
8 potato chips	110	23	20	0
ice cream bar	230	9	6	40

1. List each of the foods from the chart under the columns in which the food is listed as having more than ten grams. Some foods may be listed in more than one column.

Fat	Protein	Carbohydrates
_____	_____	_____
_____	_____	_____
_____	_____	_____
_____	_____	_____
_____	_____	_____
		_____
		_____
		_____

Name: _____ Date: _____

WEIGHTY MATTERS (cont.)

2. Of those you listed on the previous page, list the six foods that you eat the most of.

_____

_____

_____

People who have a diet that includes too much fat are in danger of developing athero-sclerosis. **Atherosclerosis** results when the arteries become clogged because of deposits of fat and cholesterol.

3. Are the foods you eat the most of high or low in fat? _____

4. How many of the calories you consume in a day should come from fat? _____

5. To maintain a healthy diet, what foods should you eat less of? More of?

_____

_____

_____

The arteries of teenagers show signs of becoming clogged if they have a diet that includes too much fat. When the arteries become clogged, the supply of blood to the heart, lungs, and brain is cut off, and a heart attack or stroke may eventually result.

In the diagram below, color in part of the artery to show the stages of developing atherosclerosis.

Artery   Age

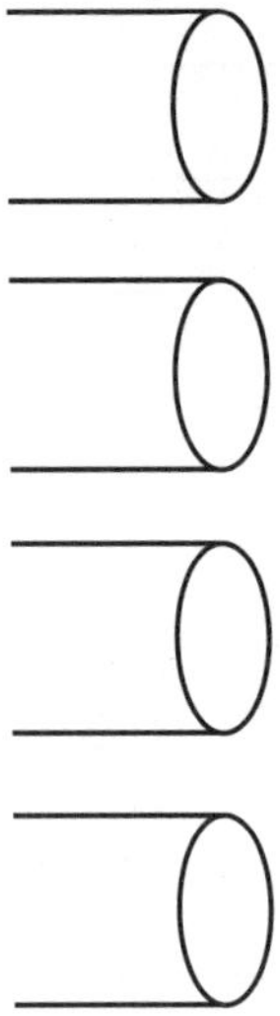

                18

                                    Decision: Eat foods that are high in saturated fats.

                30
                                    Short-term consequences:
                                        1. Fat deposit/cholesterol build-up
                                        2. Less energy

                45
                                    Long-term consequences:
                                        1. Arteries clogged
                                        2. Possible heart attack or stroke

                50

Name: _____ Date: _____

PROTEIN, CARBOHYDRATES, AND FIBER

A balanced diet is part of a healthy lifestyle. A healthy lifestyle diet includes protein, carbohydrates, and fiber. Those who eat a balanced diet usually look better, feel better, and have more energy. You must choose foods that provide protein, carbohydrates, fiber, and fat. Eating the right foods, along with exercise, is part of a healthy lifestyle.

Protein

When planning a diet, it is important to be aware that there are essential proteins and nonessential proteins. The body makes enough **nonessential proteins** to maintain good health. **Essential proteins** are known as complete proteins. They are not made by the body in sufficient quantities, so it is essential that people get them through the foods they eat. One should choose foods that are sources of essential proteins. These proteins are found in foods like eggs, meat, milk, cheese, nuts, and beans. Meat is a good source of essential protein. The best meat choices for a healthy lifestyle are fish, chicken without skin, and lean meat. The size of meat portions should be about three ounces. One must take care to not eat too much protein from meat. Weight gain and increased cholesterol levels are only two of the possible problems from eating too much meat.

Protein is important in developing and maintaining a healthy cell structure. Protein also forms most of the muscle in the body. Protein is needed to maintain body tissue and is very important in the normal growth and development of young people. Although protein is a necessary part of a nutritious diet, when one eats more than is required for a healthy diet, the excess protein is stored as fat. Storage of excess fat can result in being overweight. Maintaining the proper weight for your height and age is very important in developing a healthy lifestyle.

Name: _____ Date: _____

 # PROTEIN, CARBOHYDRATES, AND FIBER (cont.)

Protein (cont.)

proteins   meat   ounces   lean   cholesterol   nonessential   beans

When planning a diet, it is important to be aware that there are essential proteins and

1) _____ proteins. Essential proteins are known as complete proteins.

One should choose foods that are sources of essential 2) _____. These

proteins are found in foods like eggs, meat, milk, cheese,

nuts, and 3) _____. The best meat choices

for a healthy lifestyle are fish, chicken without skin, and

4) _____ meat. The size of meat portions

should be about three 5) _____.

Weight gain and increased 6) _____ levels

are only two of the possible problems from eating too much

7) _____.

fat   growth   height   overweight   protein   cell   muscle

Protein is important in developing and maintaining a healthy 8) _____

structure. Protein also forms most of the 9) _____ in the body. Protein is

needed to maintain body tissue and is very important in the normal 10) _____

and development of young people. Although 11) _____ is a necessary

part of a nutritious diet, when one eats more than is required for a healthy diet, the excess

protein is stored as 12) _____. Storage of excess fat can result in being

13) _____. Maintaining the proper weight for your 14) _____

and age is very important in a healthy lifestyle.

Name: _____ Date: _____

PROTEIN, CARBOHYDRATES, AND FIBER (cont.)

Carbohydrates

Carbohydrates are a source of energy. They also provide vitamins, minerals, and fiber in the diet. Fruits, vegetables, and whole grains found in cereals and brown bread are carbohydrates. Bread made from whole grains may range in color from black to brown. The texture of whole-grain breads is coarse. The dark color and coarse texture is because the endosperm, bran, and germ are retained as part of the bread. White bread is refined, which means the bran and germ have been removed, along with many of the vitamins, fiber, and minerals. Those who make whole-grain breads a part of their diet are less likely to be obese. They are less likely to have heart problems and diabetes. Whole-grain crackers and whole-grain foods like wild rice, brown rice, whole wheat, and whole oats are also good choices.

Read the following cloze. Complete the blanks using the words in bold.

bran   **heart**   **grain**   **germ**   **wild**   **carbohydrates**

Carbohydrates are a source of energy and provide vitamins, minerals, and fiber in the diet. Fruits, vegetables, and whole grains found in cereals and brown bread are

1) _____. Bread made from whole grains may range in color from black to brown. Additionally, the texture of whole 2) _____ breads is coarser. The dark color and coarse texture of whole-grain breads is because the endosperm,

3) _____, and germ are retained as part of the bread. White bread is refined, which means the bran and 4) _____ have been removed along with many of the vitamins, fiber, and minerals. Those who make whole-grain breads a part of their diet are less likely to be obese, have 5) _____ problems, and diabetes. In addition to whole-grain bread and crackers, whole-grain foods include

6) _____ rice, brown rice, whole wheat, and whole oats.

Name: _____ Date: _____

 # PROTEIN, CARBOHYDRATES, AND FIBER (cont.)

Fiber

Most people do not eat enough whole-grain carbohydrates. Therefore, their diet does not include enough minerals, vitamins, and fiber. Many fruits, vegetables, nuts, beans, and whole grains contain **fiber**. Although fiber should be part of a healthy diet, fiber has no food value. Fiber is important because it adds bulk to the diet. Fiber is more filling, which makes it less likely you will overeat. Fiber also aids in the passage of food through the intestines. A diet that includes fiber may help prevent diseases such as colon cancer, diabetes, and heart problems.

If you have not been getting enough fiber in your diet, you should think about eating more fruits and vegetables. When you increase the amount of fiber in your diet, you may at first experience some discomfort due to bloating and gas. However, this discomfort passes quickly as your body gets used to the new diet.

A healthy lifestyle diet includes 20 to 30 grams of fiber per day. Foods that are good sources of fiber include apples, oranges, pears, whole-wheat bread, brussels sprouts, and oatmeal.

Read the following cloze. Complete the blanks using the words in bold.

food	diet	discomfort	cancer	overeat	fiber
oatmeal	fruits	intestines	grains	grams	

Most people do not eat enough carbohydrates and therefore do not get enough minerals, vitamins, and 1) _____ in their diet. Many fruits, vegetables, nuts, beans, and whole 2) _____ contain fiber. Although fiber is an important part of a healthy diet, fiber actually has no 3) _____ value. The value of fiber is that it adds bulk to the 4) _____. Fiber is more filling, which makes it less likely you will 5) _____. Fiber also aids in the passage of food through the 6) _____. Fiber is thought to be very important in the prevention of diseases such as colon 7) _____, diabetes, and heart problems.

If you have not been getting enough fiber in your diet, you should think about adding more 8) _____ and vegetables to your diet. Those whose diet has not included enough fiber may experience some 9) _____ when increasing the amount of fiber in the diet due to bloating and gas.

A healthy lifestyle diet includes 20 to 30 10) _____ of fiber per day. Good sources of fiber include apples, oranges, pears, whole-wheat bread, brussels sprouts, and 11) _____.

Name: _____ Date: _____

NUTRIENT KNOWLEDGE

Fill in the blanks below using words and phrases found in Protein, Carbohydrates, and Fiber and in the information you have read about fats. A word or phrase may be used more than one time. Reread the Protein, Carbohydrates, and Fiber section and the Fats information if you are unsure of where to place a word or phrase.

builds muscle
source of energy
saturated in animal products
extra stored as fat
fish is a source
provides fiber
maintains body tissue

saturated and unsaturated
may prevent colon cancer
fruits and vegetables are sources
unsaturated in vegetables
milk is a source
associated with strokes

Protein	Carbohydrates	Fats

Name: _____ Date: _____

SALT AND SUGAR

It is important to very carefully monitor the amount of salt and sugar in the diet. High blood pressure can be a problem if one uses too much salt. Diabetes is often a result of eating excessive amounts of sugar.

Salt and a Healthy Lifestyle

Americans have always eaten large amounts of salt in their diet. In the early history of our country, salt was used to preserve meat and keep it from spoiling. As a result, people developed a taste for salt. Most foods today contain more than enough salt, yet the salt shaker is found on most tables. The amount of salt in a healthy diet should be limited. Too much salt often leads to high blood pressure. High blood pressure is a major cause of heart problems and stroke.

A key to limiting the amount of salt in the diet is to become a better grocery shopper. Many cheeses, packaged meats, and canned soups contain large amounts of salt. You must check the label of packaged and canned items to find the salt content. Sodium (salt) must be limited to less than 2,400 mg per day. However, eating less than 1,500 mg is even better.

> Read the following cloze. Complete the blanks using the words in bold. Some words may be used more than once.

salt   stroke   bologna   2,400   diet   spoiling   high   sodium

Excessive salt in the diet is not part of a healthy lifestyle. Americans have always included excessive amounts of **1)** _____ in their diet. In earlier times, salt was used to preserve meat and keep it from **2)** _____. As a result, the taste for salt was developed and people began to add salt to fresh foods they were eating. Even though most foods today contain more than enough salt, the salt shaker is found on most tables. To lead a healthy lifestyle, the tendency to use excess amounts of salt must be controlled. The heavy use of salt often leads to **3)** _____ blood pressure. High blood pressure often leads to heart problems and **4)** _____.

In addition to limiting the salt added to foods that you eat, it is important to become a better grocery shopper. Many cheeses, packaged meats like **5)** _____ and summer sausages, and canned soups contain large amounts of **6)** _____. Check the label of canned items for the salt content. A **7)** _____ for a healthy lifestyle should not include more than **8)** _____ mg of salt on a daily basis.

Name: _____ Date: _____

SALT AND SUGAR (cont.)

Sugar and a Healthy Lifestyle

Too much sugar in the diet is one of the main causes of obesity. Sugar is a carbohydrate. Sugar has little food value but lots of calories. This leads to weight gain. Candy, soft drinks, jams, and jellies are foods that are often very high in sugar. Any processed food may be high in sugar. Excess sugar results in increased intake of calories with little food value. A healthy lifestyle diet limits the amount of sugar. If weight loss is the goal, you must reduce the calories eaten. When trying to lose weight, one must still eat a healthy diet. To lose weight, reduce the foods that have high amounts of sugar. Eating low-fat and low-sugar foods may have a positive impact on lowering cholesterol levels, heart problems, and diabetes. However, to reduce weight, you must reduce calories. Replacing foods that are loaded with fat and sugar calories with foods that have less fat and sugar will not result in weight loss if the total calories consumed are not reduced.

> Read the following cloze. Complete the blanks using the words in bold. Some words may be used more than once.

reduced   calories   fat   sugar   diabetes   jellies   diet

Too much sugar in the diet is one of the main causes of obesity. Sugar in the diet

contributes a large amount of 1) _____ but little food value. Candy, soft

drinks, jams, 2) _____, and processed foods are often very high in

3) _____. In a healthy lifestyle 4) _____, sugar must be

limited. To lose weight, reduce the foods that have high amounts of 5) _____.

Eating low-fat and low-sugar foods may have a positive impact on lowering cholesterol levels,

heart problems, and 6) _____. However, to reduce weight, you must reduce

7) _____. Replacing foods that are loaded with fat and sugar calories with

foods that have less 8) _____ and sugar will not result in weight loss if the

calories consumed are not 9) _____.

Name: _____ Date: _____

UNDERSTANDING CHOLESTEROL, TRIGLYCERIDES, BLOOD PRESSURE, AND DIABETES

Cholesterol and Triglycerides

Cholesterol refers to fat particles carried in the bloodstream. **Lipoproteins** carry cholesterol and triglycerides to and from cells in the body. Cholesterol levels are checked using a blood test. The test gives a reading for total cholesterol, but the test should also give a reading for both LDL (low-density lipoprotein), and HDL (high-density lipoprotein). HDL and LDL are both lipoproteins. LDL circulates cholesterol in the blood, where it can build up on artery walls, leading to a disease called atherosclerosis. This can restrict blood flow and may lead to a heart attack or stroke. For this reason, LDL is often called the "bad" cholesterol. HDL is often called the "good" cholesterol. Cholesterol is carried by HDL to the liver where it does no harm. A healthy lifestyle helps lower the LDL level and increase the HDL level.

A healthy lifestyle diet limits cholesterol to 300 mg per day. The liver is the organ in our bodies that makes most of our cholesterol. We get additional cholesterol from food. Cholesterol is a fatty molecule found in animal sources such as eggs, butter, and seafood. A healthy diet tries to improve our good cholesterol and lower our bad cholesterol. Oatmeal is a food that lowers cholesterol. Foods from soybeans, called soy foods, have been found to lower cholesterol. Salmon, mackerel, and herring are rich in omega-3 fatty acids, which are recommended to improve cholesterol and triglyceride levels.

Understanding the ratio between HDL and LDL:	
Total Cholesterol:	below 200 is desirable
LDL Cholesterol:	below 100 is desirable
HDL Cholesterol:	above 60 is desirable

Triglycerides are the fats found in your blood. Any calories eaten that are not used for energy are changed to triglycerides and stored as fat in the body. Triglycerides are important for your health, but it is recommended that your triglycerides be below 150. When triglycerides get higher than 150, it is a danger signal that you may have a better chance to develop heart problems. A blood test shows your triglyceride level.

If you eat more calories than you need, it is likely you will become overweight as the extra triglycerides are stored in your body as fat. A triglyceride reading above 150 is often found in those who are overweight. Exercising, not eating more calories than you need, and watching the amount of saturated fat in your diet are important in maintaining a triglyceride level below 150. In some cases, it may be necessary to take medication to bring high triglycerides under control.

Triglycerides	
Desirable:	150 or below
Concern:	150 to 200
Extreme:	200 and above

Name: _____ Date: _____

UNDERSTANDING CHOLESTEROL, TRIGLYCERIDES, BLOOD PRESSURE, AND DIABETES (cont.)

Cholesterol and Triglycerides (cont.)

Read the cloze below. Complete the blanks using the words below.

bad	**fat**	**deposits**	**liver**	**diet**	**blood**	**good**
lipoproteins	**cholesterol**					

Cholesterol refers to a form of **1)** _____ carried in the bloodstream. Lipoproteins carry cholesterol and triglycerides to and from cells in the body. The **2)** _____ level is checked using a blood test. Normally, a cholesterol test gives a reading for total cholesterol, low-density lipoprotein (LDL), and high-density lipoprotein (HDL). HDL and LDL are both **3)** _____. A high reading for LDL means that fatty **4)** _____ may be building on the walls of the arteries. The fatty deposits will restrict **5)** _____ flow through the arteries, which leads to heart attack or stroke. For this reason, LDL is often called the **6)** "_____" cholesterol. HDL is often called the **7)** "_____" cholesterol. HDL carries cholesterol away from the arteries to the **8)** _____ where it is eliminated with no harm. A healthy lifestyle **9)** _____ is recommended to lower the LDL cholesterol level and increase the HDL cholesterol level.

heart	**medication**	**fats**	**Exercising**	**calories**	**saturated**
overweight		**150**			

Triglycerides are the **10)** _____ found in your blood. It is important that your triglycerides are below **11)** _____. When triglycerides get higher than 150, it is a danger signal that you may have a better chance to develop **12)** _____ problems. If you eat more **13)** _____ than you need, it is likely you will become overweight. A high triglyceride reading above 150 is often found in those who are **14)** _____. **15)** _____, not eating more calories than you need, and watching the amount of **16)** _____ fat in your diet are important in maintaining a triglyceride level below 150. In some cases, it may be necessary to take **17)** _____ to bring high triglycerides under control.

Name: _____ Date: _____

UNDERSTANDING CHOLESTEROL, TRIGLYCERIDES, BLOOD PRESSURE, AND DIABETES (cont.)

Blood Pressure and a Healthy Lifestyle

A healthy lifestyle helps you control weight and feel better and gives you more energy. A healthy lifestyle diet can also improve cholesterol levels and reduce blood pressure. High cholesterol and high blood pressure levels make heart problems and strokes more likely.

When the heart beats, blood is pushed through the arteries. Blood is also moving through the arteries between beats, when the heart is at rest. If the arteries are blocked, then the heart must pump harder. A **blood pressure reading** gives two numbers, such as 120/80. The top number, called **systolic pressure**, is the blood pressure when the heart is beating. The bottom number, called **diastolic pressure**, is the blood pressure when the heart is at rest between beats. The higher the blood pressure numbers, the more difficult it is for blood to move through your arteries. This causes the heart to work harder. High blood pressure is a primary cause of heart problems and strokes. People of all ages should monitor blood pressure levels. Blood pressure may vary from time to time. It is best to take a number of readings and find the average. This will give you a more accurate blood pressure reading.

Normal Blood Pressure: Lower than 120/80
Elevated Blood Pressure: Above 120/80 to 139/89
High Blood Pressure: 140/90 and above

Complete the following blanks

1. When the heart beats, blood is pushed through the _____.

2. Blood is moving through the arteries when the heart is beating and at _____.

3. A blood pressure reading gives _____ numbers, such as 120/80.

4. The top number, called _____ pressure, is the blood pressure when the heart is beating.

5. The bottom number, called _____ pressure, is the blood pressure when the heart is at rest between beats.

6. The higher the blood pressure numbers, the more _____ it is for blood to move through the arteries.

7. High blood pressure is a primary cause of heart problems and _____.

8. Blood pressure may vary from time to time, so it is best to take a number of readings and find the _____.

9. A normal blood pressure reading would be _____/_____ and lower.

10. A high blood pressure reading would be _____/_____ and above.

UNDERSTANDING CHOLESTEROL, TRIGLYCERIDES, BLOOD PRESSURE, AND DIABETES (cont.)

Diabetes and a Healthy Lifestyle

Diabetes is a disease that effects both children and adults. **Diabetes** occurs when insulin is either not produced properly or not used properly by the body. **Insulin** is a hormone that regulates the levels of glucose, or sugar, in the body's cells. When there is a problem with the insulin in the body, the glucose cannot get into the cells, and the level of glucose in the blood increases to a dangerous level.

Type 1 diabetes usually develops in childhood or adolescence. It is the form of diabetes where the body is not able to make enough insulin, which leads to high blood glucose levels. Type 1 diabetes is managed with injections of insulin.

Type 2 diabetes is the most common form of diabetes. In this form, the body is not able to properly use insulin, which leads to high blood glucose. It is generally more common among people who are over 35 years of age. Typically, the person with Type 2 diabetes is inactive and overweight. Today, many young people are overweight because they do not eat a healthy lifestyle diet. As a result, the occurrence of Type 2 diabetes has been increasing among young people. It is estimated that millions of people have Type 2 diabetes, and many of those do not know they are diabetic. Type 2 diabetes can be managed with diet and exercise, although pills to increase insulin production or decrease glucose in the blood and injections of insulin may also be needed.

The test for diabetes is a blood test that checks the glucose level. A high level of glucose (above 125 milligrams glucose per deciliter of drawn blood) may indicate a diabetic condition. Some of the symptoms of diabetes include a frequent thirst, weight loss, tiredness, and slow healing of cuts and bruises. Diabetes can lead to heart problems, stroke, blindness, kidney disease, circulation problems, and in many cases, amputation of limbs.

One of the best ways to prevent diabetes is to maintain a weight that is appropriate for one's age and height. Fiber is an important part of a diet that helps control diabetes. Fiber can help lower the blood sugar for those with Type 2 diabetes.

Type 2 Diabetes Checklist

There are symptoms that may indicate you should be checked for diabetes. Some of the common symptoms are listed below. Place a check on the blank if the statement applies to you.

_____ 1. I am overweight.   _____ 2. I am often thirsty.

_____ 3. I do not have a daily exercise program.   _____ 4. I am often tired.

_____ 5. I have family members with diabetes.   _____ 6. I must urinate frequently.

_____ 7. I have wounds that heal slowly.   _____ 8. I often eat large meals.

_____ 9. I am African-American or Hispanic.   _____ 10. I often skip meals.

_____ 11. My diet does not include 30–50 grams of fiber per day.

_____ 12. My diet does not include fruits and vegetables each day.

Name: _____ Date: _____

ASSESSING WHAT HAS BEEN LEARNED

Assessment 1: Matching

Match the words below with the correct meanings. Write the letter of the word on the blank by the correct meaning.

a. cholesterol   b. systolic   c. polyunsaturated   d. monounsaturated
e. arteries   f. diastolic   g. diabetes   h. antioxidants
i. saturated   j. glucose   k. lipoproteins   l. trans fats
m. lycopene   n. triglycerides

_____ 1. Fats found in meat and dairy products. Eating too much of this fat leads to higher cholesterol.

_____ 2. Fats found in foods like olive oil, peanut oil, and canola oil. This fat is necessary to help the body build stronger cells.

_____ 3. Fats found in foods like nuts, seeds, corn, and soybeans. This fat is also necessary to help build stronger cells.

_____ 4. Fat found in processed foods like margarine and shortenings. These hydrogenated fats increase the bad cholesterol level. These fats should not be part of the diet.

_____ 5. Blood moves through these from the heart to other parts of the body

_____ 6. Blood pressure reading when the heart is pumping. The top number on a blood pressure reading.

_____ 7. Blood pressure reading when the heart is at rest, or between beats. The bottom number on a blood pressure reading.

_____ 8. Both LDL, which is "bad" cholesterol, and HDL, which is "good" cholesterol.

_____ 9. Fats that travel in the blood stream.

_____ 10. Nutrients that keep free radicals from damaging our body's cells.

_____ 11. One of the fats that help build cells and is a source of energy. Too much of this in the blood forms deposits on the walls of the arteries.

_____ 12. Refers to blood sugar. Glucose in the blood is tested to check for diabetes. A high glucose level may indicate diabetes.

_____ 13. Occurs when the level of glucose in the blood is too high, indicating glucose is not getting to the cells.

_____ 14. Antioxidant found in tomatoes.

Name: _____ Date: _____

ASSESSING WHAT HAS BEEN LEARNED (cont.)

Assessment 2: Word Choice

From the two words given, choose the word to which each sentence refers. Circle the correct word.

1. This is found in eggs, milk, and meat and is important in building muscle.

   protein   carbohydrates

2. This is found in fruits, vegetables, and grains and provides vitamins and bulk in the diet.

   protein   carbohydrates

3. This food in the diet adds bulk, but it has no food value.

   fiber   sugar

4. This food is an important source of energy, but if your diet contains too much, you will likely become overweight.

   fat   fiber

5. The test for this is to check the level of glucose (sugar) in the blood.

   cholesterol   diabetes

6. A fatty substance carried in the blood stream.

   cholesterol   chromosomes

7. These small fat particles are one of the fats in the blood.

   triglycerides   arteries

8. If there is too much cholesterol in the blood, these often become clogged with fat deposits.

   triglycerides   arteries

9. The blood pressure reading when the heart is pumping.

   diastolic   systolic

10. The blood pressure reading when the heart is resting.

    diastolic   systolic

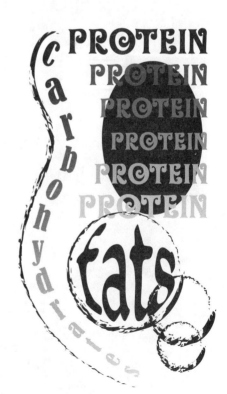

Name: _____ Date: _____

 # ASSESSING WHAT HAS BEEN LEARNED (cont.)

Assessment 3: Crossword Puzzle

Complete the crossword puzzle using the clues on page 23.

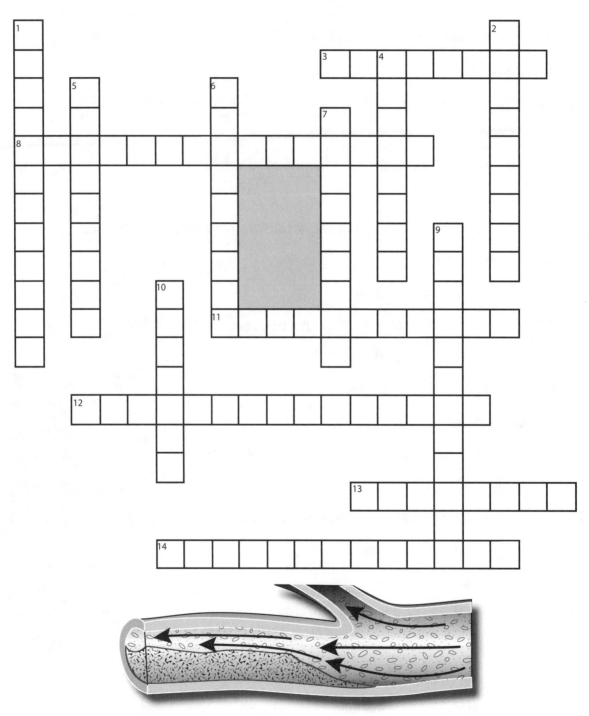

The blood flow in this artery is being blocked by fatty deposits.

Name: _____ Date: _____

ASSESSING WHAT HAS BEEN LEARNED (cont.)

Assessment 3: Crossword Puzzle (cont.)

Complete the crossword puzzle on page 22 using the clues below. The phonetic pronunciations for the words are given to help you.

ACROSS

3. (dī-ə-bē-təs): Occurs when the level of glucose in the blood is too high, indicating that the glucose is not getting to the cells

8. (pä-lē-ən-sa-chə-rā-təd): Fats found in foods like nuts, seeds, corn, and soybeans. This fat is necessary to help the body build stronger cells.

11. (kə-les-tə-rōl): One of the fats that travels in the bloodstream and helps build cells and provides a source of energy. Too much of this in the blood forms deposits on the walls of the arteries.

12. (mä-nō-ən-sa-chə-rā-təd): Fats found in foods like olive oil, peanut oil, and canola oil. This fat is necessary to help the body build stronger cells.

13. (sis-tä-lik): Blood pressure reading when the heart is pumping (the top number)

14. (trī-gli-sə-rīdz): Fats found in most foods and in the body in the bloodstream. Calories that are not used are changed to this and stored as fat in the body.

DOWN

1. (lī-pō prō-tēnz): Proteins that carry all the different kinds of cholesterol in the blood.

2. (de-sə-lē-tər): One tenth of a liter (1/10)

4. (är-tə-rēz): Blood vessels that move blood from the heart to other parts of the body

5. (mi-lə-gram): One thousandth of a gram (1/1,000)

6. (dī-ə-stä-lik): Blood pressure reading when the heart is at rest between beats (the bottom number)

7. (sa-chə-rā-təd): Fats found in meat and dairy products. Eating too much of this fat leads to higher cholesterol.

9. (hī-drä-jə-nā-təd): Fat found in processed foods like baked goods and shortening. It has had hydrogen artificially added. It increases the bad cholesterol level.

10. (glü-kōs): Refers to blood sugar. High levels of this in the blood may indicate diabetes.

Name: _____ Date: _____

THE FOOD PYRAMID AND A HEALTHY LIFESTYLE

The Food Pyramid

Everyone should try to include more fruits, vegetables, unsaturated fats, and whole grains in their diets. The amount of sugar and salt should be limited. The **Food Guide Pyramid** created by the United States Department of Agriculture (USDA) and the Department of Health and Human Services (HHS) lists the following recommended serving sizes and number of servings from each food group.

Recommended Servings Per Day: $2\frac{1}{2}$ cups of vegetables per day
2 cups of fruit
3 cups of milk
6 ounces of grains
$5\frac{1}{2}$ ounces of protein, found in foods like meat, nuts, and beans

Examples of Serving Sizes From Each Food Group:

Breads, Rice, Cereals, and Pasta
1 slice of bread; 1 ounce of ready-to-eat cereal; $\frac{1}{2}$ cup of cooked cereal, pasta, or rice

Vegetables
1 cup of raw leafy vegetables; $\frac{1}{2}$ cup of cooked vegetables; $\frac{3}{4}$ cup of vegetable juice

Fruits
1 medium apple, banana, or orange; $\frac{1}{2}$ cup of chopped, cooked, or canned fruit; $\frac{3}{4}$ cup of fruit juice

Protein
2 to 3 ounces of cooked lean meat or poultry; $\frac{1}{2}$ cup of cooked dry beans; 1 egg; $\frac{1}{3}$ cup of nuts

Name: _____ Date: _____

THE FOOD PYRAMID AND A HEALTHY LIFESTYLE (cont.)

Making a record of the foods you eat is a good way to determine if you are eating the recommended number of servings from the food groups. Write the food you ate and the amount of the food in the appropriate blanks below each of the food groups. Keep the record for three days. After each day, complete the statement following the daily record. Check your choices online at the USDA Food Pyramid Guide at www.mypyramid.gov to learn more about recommended daily servings from each of the food groups.

Day 1

Breads, Rice, Cereals, Pasta	Vegetables	Fruits	Protein
_____	_____	_____	_____
_____	_____	_____	_____
_____	_____	_____	_____
_____	_____	_____	_____
_____	_____	_____	_____

I need more servings from _____.

Day 2

Breads, Rice, Cereals, Pasta	Vegetables	Fruits	Protein
_____	_____	_____	_____
_____	_____	_____	_____
_____	_____	_____	_____
_____	_____	_____	_____
_____	_____	_____	_____

I need more servings from _____.

Day 3

Breads, Rice, Cereals, Pasta	Vegetables	Fruits	Protein
_____	_____	_____	_____
_____	_____	_____	_____
_____	_____	_____	_____
_____	_____	_____	_____
_____	_____	_____	_____

I need more servings from _____.

Name: _____ Date: _____

DAILY RECOMMENDED CALORIC INTAKE

Calories

The foods we eat are important if we want to lead a healthy lifestyle. One of the first steps we must take is limiting the total calories we consume each day. The number of recommended calories per day is based on one's level of activity. It is a general recommendation for normal activity that women limit calorie intake to between 1,600 and 2,000 per day. Men should limit calorie intake to between 2,000 and 2,500 per day. Young children or those who are inactive need to adjust their caloric intake accordingly.

If you eat more calories than you burn, you will gain weight even while eating a healthy diet. Therefore, to reduce weight, you must eat a healthy diet and not eat more calories than are needed on a daily basis.

It is important to think about the amount of food and the kind of foods that make up our daily calorie intake. The calories that make up our daily diet should be chosen for their fat, carbohydrate, and fiber content. Choose fruits and vegetables from the various color groups. These foods are loaded with fiber and vitamins. Make sure your diet includes whole grains and beans. In selecting fats, you must limit foods with saturated fats or trans fats.

The chart below shows the recommended amounts of the fats, carbohydrates, and fiber, as well as sodium and cholesterol, that should make up a 2,000-calorie and 2,500-calorie diet.

Recommended Daily Diet:	2,000 calories	2,500 calories
Total fat: less than	65 g	80 g
Saturated fat: less than	20 g	25 g
Cholesterol: less than	300 mg	300 mg
Sodium: less than	2,400 mg	2,400 mg
Total Carbohydrates:	300 g	375 g
Dietary Fiber:	25 g	30 g

Circle the answers that correctly complete each sentence below.

1. The amount of total fat in the 2,500-calorie diet should be   a) 80 mg.   b) 65 g.
   c) 80 g.   d) 65 mg.

2. The amount of saturated fat in the 2,500-calorie diet should be less than   a) 20 g.
   b) 20 mg.   c) 25 g.   d) 25 mg.

3. In both diets, it is recommended that the intake of sodium be   a) more than
   b) less than   2,400 mg.

4. In both diets, the amount of   a) cholesterol   b) saturated fat   c) total fat   is 300 mg.

5. When the diet increases from 2,000 calories to 2,500 calories, the amount of dietary fiber recommended increases by   a) 5   b) 10   c) 15   d) 20   grams.

Name: _____ Date: _____

ALL YOU CAN EAT

1. In this exercise, assume that 2,400 calories are needed each day to provide the proper amount of energy without gaining weight. Choose the foods that you will eat to get the 2,400 calories. You may not eat more, or you will store the excess energy as fat and gain weight. Beside each food is listed the calories contained in a serving. Put a check by the foods that you will eat today to consume the 2,400 calories.

_____ Hot dog–124	_____ Peas ($\frac{1}{2}$ cup)–70
_____ Milk (1 cup)–165	_____ Soda (12 ounces)–160
_____ Fried chicken ($\frac{1}{4}$ pound)–275	_____ French fries (12)–210
_____ Turkey ($\frac{1}{4}$ pound)–270	_____ Milk shake (16 ounces)–420
_____ Egg–75	_____ Chocolate bar–160
_____ Vegetable soup (1 cup)–90	_____ Ice cream (scoop)–270
_____ Apple–75	_____ Ice cream sandwich–260
_____ Banana–90	_____ Doughnut (plain)–140
_____ Grapes ($\frac{1}{2}$ cup)–65	_____ Bagel–125
_____ Orange–75	_____ Cereal ($\frac{3}{4}$ cup)–100
_____ Pear–95	_____ Orange juice (1 cup)–100
_____ Peaches (canned, 2 halves)–90	_____ Hamburger ($\frac{1}{4}$ pound) on bun–410
_____ Kidney beans ($\frac{1}{2}$ cup)–90	_____ Pizza (cheese, 3 slices)–400
_____ Carrots ($\frac{1}{2}$ cup)–35	_____ Tossed salad (1 cup)–120
_____ Broccoli ($\frac{1}{2}$ cup)–30	_____ Chicken noodle soup (1 cup)–65
_____ Corn ($\frac{1}{2}$ cup)–75	_____ Baked potato (large)–130
_____ Potato chips (eight chips)–110	_____ Rice ($\frac{3}{4}$ cup)–150
_____ Fruit cocktail ($\frac{1}{2}$ cup)–100	_____ Spaghetti (1 cup)–230
_____ Cheese (1 ounce)–115	_____ Macaroni ($\frac{3}{4}$ cup)–120
_____ Lettuce (1 cup)–20	

Answer the following.

2. Looking at the food pyramid on page 24, my diet includes foods from all of the pyramid food groups. _____ yes _____ no

3. In choosing a healthy lifestyle meal, it is important to watch the number of _____ in the meal.

4. Most of the foods in my daily diet are chosen from the **a)** vegetable **b)** fruit **c)** grain **d)** protein group.

5. I need to eat more foods from the **a)** vegetable **b)** fruit **c)** grain **d)** protein group.

Name: _____ Date: _____

NUTRITIONAL FAVORITES

It is important to eat properly and exercise if you want to stay healthy. Good nutrition and exercise do not guarantee that everyone will stay healthy and have a good lifestyle; however, it can be said that those who exercise and eat properly do usually look better, feel better, and have more energy.

This exercise is designed to help you determine whether or not you eat nutritional foods. Place a plus (+) by the foods that you eat most often and a minus (-) by the ones that you hardly ever eat.

_____ 1. hamburger	_____ 2. carrots	_____ 3. pizza
_____ 4. baked potato	_____ 5. french fries	_____ 6. donut
_____ 7. beans	_____ 8. orange juice	_____ 9. soda
_____ 10. candy bar	_____ 11. banana	_____ 12. tomato juice
_____ 13. broccoli	_____ 14. apple	_____ 15. pie
_____ 16. potato chips	_____ 17. salad	_____ 18. hot dog
_____ 19. cheese	_____ 20. nachos/cheese	

The food pyramid below lists the foods that we should eat each day to have a nutritional diet. Put a plus (+) in the part of the pyramid that represents each of the foods above that you put a plus by. Then lightly shade the part of the pyramid that represents the foods that you eat the most.

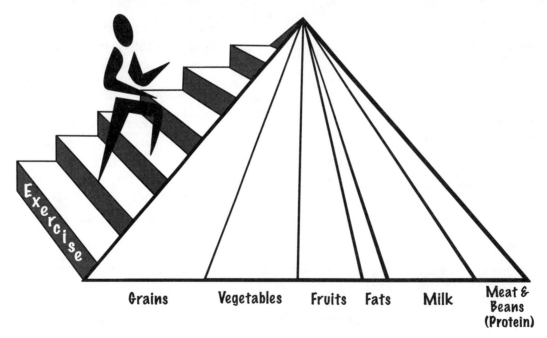

What foods do you think you need to eat more of? less of? _____

_____

Name: _____ Date: _____

DIET DILEMMA

Good nutrition and a healthy lifestyle are best maintained by using the diet recommended in the food pyramid. Trying to maintain a healthy lifestyle by consuming more vitamins and minerals than is recommended and going on fad diets may be detrimental to your health.

In choosing a nutritious diet, it is important to know in which part of the food pyramid different foods are found. Use the food pyramid and place the letters of the pyramid sections in the blanks before each of the following foods, indicating the food group in which each is found.

_____ **1.** orange	_____ **2.** hamburger	_____ **3.** milk
_____ **4.** oatmeal	_____ **5.** cabbage	_____ **6.** chicken
_____ **7.** cheese	_____ **8.** peanut butter	_____ **9.** potato
_____ **10.** hot dog	_____ **11.** butter	_____ **12.** broccoli
_____ **13.** banana	_____ **14.** beans	_____ **15.** sausage
_____ **16.** lettuce	_____ **17.** celery	_____ **18.** rice
_____ **19.** bread	_____ **20.** apple	

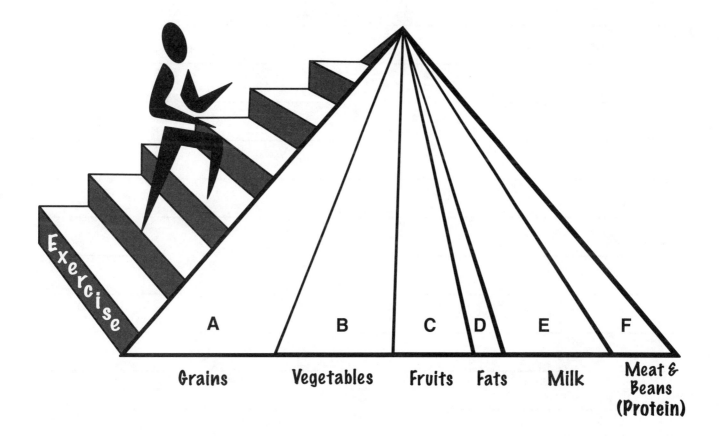

Name: _____ Date: _____

DIET DILEMMA (cont.)

A well-balanced diet should be chosen from the five food groups. When a diet is chosen from the five food groups, the diet should be planned around the recommended daily allowances of fats, sodium, carbohydrates, and fiber.

Choose foods from each food group and plan a diet for one day. Choose foods you think you would like, but try to plan a balanced diet. Then determine if your diet is within the recommended daily allowances for each of the nutrients shown on the chart below.

Recommended Daily Diet:	2,000 calories	2,500 calories
Total fat: less than	65 g	80 g
Saturated fat: less than	20 g	25 g
Cholesterol: less than	300 mg	300 mg
Sodium: less than	2,400 mg	2,400 mg
Total Carbohydrates:	300 g	375 g
Dietary Fiber:	25 g	30 g

List the foods in your diet plan for one day. Include breakfast, lunch, dinner, and two snacks.

_____

_____

_____

_____

_____

_____

_____

_____

_____

_____

Name: _____ Date: _____

 # USING MATH TO UNDERSTAND FOOD LABELS

Understanding Metric Measurement Prefixes

In the metric system, the liter is the metric measurement for liquid. Meter is a metric measurement for length. Gram is a metric measurement for weight. The prefixes deci-, centi-, and milli- are used to compare metric measurements. The deci-, centi-, and milli- prefixes are used in metric measurements for liquid, length, and weight.

deci- means 1/10   centi- means 1/100   milli- means 1/1,000

Choose the correct answer to complete each statement.

1. A deciliter is 1/10 of a   a) meter.   b) liter.   c) gram.
2. A decimeter is 1/10 of a   a) meter.   b) liter.   c) gram.
3. A decigram is 1/10 of   a) meter.   b) liter.   c) gram.
4. A centiliter is 1/100 of a   a) meter.   b) liter.   c) gram.
5. A centimeter is 1/100 of a   a) meter.   b) liter.   c) gram.
6. A centigram is 1/100 of   a) meter.   b) liter.   c) gram.
7. A milliliter is 1/1,000 of a   a) meter.   b) liter.   c) gram.
8. A millimeter is 1/1,000 of a   a) meter.   b) liter.   c) gram.
9. A milligram is 1/1,000 of a   a) meter.   b) liter.   c) gram.

Comparing the Common Metric Measurements Liter, Deciliter, Centiliter, and Milliliter

deci- means 1/10   centi- means 1/100   milli- means 1/1,000
One liter equals 10 deciliters; 100 centiliters; 1,000 milliliters.
10 milliliters = 1 centiliter   10 centiliters = 1 deciliter   10 deciliters = 1 liter
1 milliliter = 0.034 ounces

Choose the correct answer to complete each statement.

1.   It takes   a) 10   b) 100   c) 1,000   deciliters to make a liter.
2.   It takes   a) 10   b) 100   c) 1,000   centiliters to make a liter.
3.   It takes   a) 10   b) 100   c) 1,000   milliliters to make a liter.
4.   It takes   a) 1   b) 2   c) 5   d) 8   deciliters to make $\frac{1}{2}$ a liter
5.   It takes   a) 50   b) 40   c) 30   d) 20   centiliters to make $\frac{1}{2}$ a liter.
6.   It takes   a) 100   b) 200   c) 500   d) 800   milliliters to make $\frac{1}{2}$ a liter.
7.   A deciliter is equal to   a) 1/10   b) 1/100   c) 1/1,000   of a liter.
8.   A deciliter is equal to   a) 3.4   b) 0.34   c) 0.034   ounces.
9.   A centiliter is equal to   a) 1/10   b) 1/100   c) 1/1,000   of a liter.
10. A centiliter is equal to   a) 3.4   b) 0.34   c) 0.034   ounces.
11. A milliliter is equal to   a) 1/10   b) 1/100   c) 1/1,000   of a liter.
12. A milliliter is equal to   a) 3.4   b) 0.34   c) 0.034   ounces.

Name: _____ Date: _____

USING MATH TO UNDERSTAND FOOD LABELS (cont.)

Most food labels use the metric system to indicate the amount of nutrients contained in the food. The following exercises will help you understand the metric system when analyzing a food label.

Metric Measurement for Health

Compare liters, deciliters, centiliters, and milliliters with gallons and quarts. The liter is a metric measurement that can be compared to a quart. A fluid (liquid) liter equals 1.057 fluid quarts. Another way of comparing a liter and quart is to say that a fluid quart is 0.946 of a fluid liter.

> Choose or supply the correct answer to complete each of the following statements.

1. One liter equals 1.057 quarts, so a liter is (more / less) than a quart.

2. Two liters equals 2 • 1.057 = _____ quarts.

3. Three liters equals 3 • 1.057 = _____ quarts.

4. Four liters equals 4 • 1.057= _____ quarts.

5. Four liters is (more / less) than a gallon.

6. Since 0.946 liters equals one quart, a liter is (more / less) than a quart.

7. Since the decimal 0.946 is (more / less) than 1, you know the liter is (larger / smaller) than a quart.

8. Because 0.946 liters equals one quart, one gallon would equal

    a) 1.892   **b)** 2.838   **c)** 3.784   **d)** 4. 73   liters.

A quart is equal to four cups. A cup is equal to eight ounces. Therefore, a quart is 32 ounces. A liter is equal to four and one-fourth cups.

9. A liter is equal to   **a)** 30   **b)** 32   **c)** 34   **d)** 36   ounces.

10. A gallon is equal to four quarts, or 128 ounces. A gallon is equal to

    a) 4.25   **b)** 2.89   **c)** 5.1   **d)** 3.784   liters.

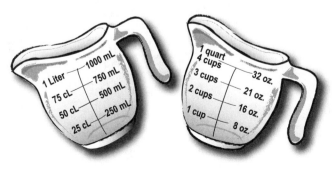

Name: _____ Date: _____

USING MATH TO UNDERSTAND FOOD LABELS (cont.)

Comparing Grams and Kilograms to Ounces and Pounds

When buying food at the store, the food labels may list the weight and content of various fats, carbohydrates, and fiber using ounces and pounds or grams and kilograms.

16 ounces (oz.) = 1 pound (lb.)   1,000 grams (g) = 1 kilogram (kg)
1,000 milligrams (mg) = 1 gram   453.5 grams = 1 pound
1 ounce = 28.35 grams   1 kilogram = 2.2 pounds

Choose the correct answer to complete each statement.

1. A food label that lists the weight as 4 kilograms would weigh
    a) 2.2   b) 8.8   c) 2   d) 8   pounds.

2. A food label that lists a weight as 1.1 pounds would weigh
    a) $\frac{1}{2}$ b) 1   c) $1\frac{1}{2}$ d) 2   kilogram(s).

3. A sack of sugar weighs 4.54 kilograms. The weight in pounds is
    approximately   a) 8.8   b) 9.5   c) 10   d) 12   pounds.

4. The label on a sack of prunes shows the weight as 500 grams. The sack of prunes weighs
    a) $\frac{1}{4}$ b) $\frac{1}{2}$ c) $\frac{3}{4}$ d) $\frac{5}{6}$ of a kilogram.

5. The label on bags of candy shows the weight as 453 grams. You know the weight is
    approximately   a) 1   b) 2   c) 3   d) 4   pound(s).

6. The weight on a can is shown as 750 grams. The can weighs
    a) $\frac{1}{4}$ b) $\frac{1}{2}$ c) $\frac{3}{4}$ d) $\frac{5}{6}$ of a kilogram.

7. Ten pounds would be   a) 2.2   b) 4.54   c) 12.2   d) 22   kilograms.

8. A food item that weighs 5 kilograms would weigh
    a) 2,000   b) 3,000   c) 4,000   d) 5,000   grams.

9. A food item that weighs four ounces would weigh approximately
    a) 90   b) 100   c) 113   d) 123   grams.

10. A food item that weighs 227 grams weighs approximately
    a) $\frac{1}{4}$ b) $\frac{1}{2}$ c) $\frac{3}{4}$ d) $\frac{5}{6}$ of a pound.

11. You go to the store to buy $\frac{1}{4}$ pound of sugar. The weight on the sugar is shown in grams.
    You would buy the sugar with a label weight of
    a) 83   b) 93   c) 103   d) 113   grams.

12. The label on a food item shows the weight as 1,500 grams.
    You know the weight is   a) $\frac{1}{2}$ b) 1   c) $1\frac{1}{2}$ d) 2   kilograms.

13. A scale shows that the weight is 3 kilograms.
    The weight is   a) 3.6   b) 4.6   c) 5.6   d) 6.6   pounds.

14. The fat content in cookies is listed as 14 grams.
    This is approximately   a) $\frac{1}{4}$ b) $\frac{1}{2}$ c) $\frac{3}{4}$ d) 1   ounce.

Name: _____ Date: _____

USING MATH TO UNDERSTAND FOOD LABELS (cont.)

Assessment 4: Metric Measurements of Mass

Fill in the answers in the following.

1. mg = _____   kg = _____   g = _____

2. 1,000 milligrams = 1 _____   1,000 grams = 1 _____

3. One kilogram equals _____ pounds.

4. One ounce equals approximately _____ grams.

5. It takes approximately _____ grams to equal one-half pound.

6. Complete the following chart.

    1,000 g = 1 kilogram   1 kilogram = 2.2 pounds
    454 g = 1 pound   1 pound = 0.454 kilograms

Ounces	1	2	3	4	5	6	7	8	9
Grams	28.35	56.7	85.05	113.4		170.1	198.45		255.15

Ounces	10	11	12	13	14	15	16
Grams	283.5		340.2	368.55		425.25	453.6

7. Complete the blanks for kilograms

Pounds	2.2	4.4	6.6	8.8	11.0	13.2	15.4	17.6	19.8	22.0
Kilograms										

USING MATH TO UNDERSTAND FOOD LABELS (cont.)

Understanding Percentages

To understand food labels, you must understand percentages. The word *percent* means "per hundred." Most of the time, the food label will list the percentage of a particular ingredient as the percentage of daily requirements. For example, an ingredient like sugar might be listed as 10 g, which is 10% of one's daily requirement.

To change a number to percent, you must first determine where the decimal is located in a number. In whole numbers like 1, 2, 3, 4, 5, etc., the decimal is located after the whole number. 1.0, 2.0, 3,0, 4.0, 5.0. But there are also numbers like 1.24, 2.78, 4.67, 0.45, 0.08, and 0.0034. All of these numbers can be changed to a percent. After you find the decimal point, move the decimal point two places to the right and add a percent sign.

Examples: 1 = 1.0 = 100. = 100%	2.78 = 278. = 278%
0.08 = 8. = 8%	0.0034 = 0.34 = 0.34%

1. Change each of the following to a percent.

   a) 2.0 becomes _____%   b) 3.0 becomes _____%

   c) 4.0 becomes _____%   d) 5.0 becomes _____%.

   e) 2.78 becomes _____%   f) 3.08 becomes _____%

   g) 4.67 becomes _____%   h) 0.45 becomes _____%

   i) 0.04 becomes _____%   j) 0.0068 becomes _____%.

2. You must read percentages carefully. The number 0.0034 changed to a percent becomes 0.34%. This is less than 1% because the decimal 0.34% is read as thirty-four hundredths percent.

   Place a plus sign (+) on the blank if the percent is greater than 1%.

   a) ____ 25%   b) ____ 0.12%   c) ____ 0.04%   d) ____ 67%

   e) ____ 89%   f) ____ 0.56%   g) ____ 0.005%

USING MATH TO UNDERSTAND FOOD LABELS (cont.)

Finding the Percentage

To find the percent of a given number, first change the percent to a decimal. Then multiply the decimal times the given number.

> **Example:** Find 30% of 50. Change 30% to the decimal 0.30 and multiply 0.30 times 50.
>
> $$\begin{array}{r} 50 \\ \times\ 0.30 \\ \hline 0\ 00 \\ 1\ 50 \\ \hline 15.00 \end{array}$$

Solve the following.

1. 20% of 100 = _____

2. 35% of 50 = _____

3. 40% of 500 = _____

4. 25% of 2,000 = _____

5. 15% of 1,600 = _____

6. 30% of 150 = _____

7. 22% of 75 = _____

8. 85% of 30 = _____

9. 67% of 400 = _____

10. 6% of 92 = _____

Name: _____ Date: _____

FOOD LABELS

Understanding Food Labels

When shopping for food, you must read the food labels. Reading the food label carefully will help you make good choices. Food labels list valuable information. One of the first things on the label is the number of calories. Calories are usually listed per serving. Therefore, it is important to note how many servings you can get from a package. The label will tell you the total amount of fat. It is important to note the amount of the total fat that is saturated fat. The food label will also list the % Daily Value. This tells you what percent a listed item on the label is of your total daily needs.

This is a label you might find on a food you are buying. Read the following label and answer the questions.

Food Label 1	Nutrition Facts	2,000-calorie diet
Serving size	2 tsp. 32 g	
Calories 190	Calories from fat 140	
		% Daily Value
Total fat	17g	26%
Saturated fat	3.6 g	18%
Trans fat	0 g	
Cholesterol	0 mg	
Sodium	144 mg	6%
Total Carbohydrates	6 g	2%
Dietary fiber	2 g	8%
Sugar	3 g	
Protein	7 g	

Fill in the blanks with answers that correctly complete each statement.

1. The letter "g" following an ingredient means _____.

2. The letters "mg" following an ingredient means _____.

3. The ingredient "saturated fat" is listed as _____ grams.

4. The amount of saturated fat is _____% of one's daily requirement for saturated fat.

5. The ingredient dietary fiber is listed as _____ grams.

6. The amount of dietary fiber is _____% of one's daily requirement for dietary fiber.

Name: _____ Date: _____

FOOD LABELS (cont.)

Finding Your Daily Requirement

A food label shows that an ingredient is a certain percent of one's daily requirement. You can find the total daily requirement for the ingredient by dividing the amount of the ingredient listed by the decimal of the daily requirement.

> **Example:** Let's say 17 g is 26% of one's total daily requirement of fat for a 2,000-calorie diet.
>
> Let x represent the total daily requirement of fat.
>
> **Step 1:** To find x, we must change 26% back to a decimal.
> **Step 2:** To do this, you move the decimal point two places to the left, so 26% becomes 0.26.
> **Step 3:** Now set up the problem as 17 g ÷ 0.26 = x
> **Step 4:** Divide 17 g ÷ 0.26 = 65 g. This amount is the total daily requirement of fat for a 2,000-calorie diet.

Solve the following.

1. Food Label 1 shows that there are 144 mg of sodium, which is 6% of one's total daily requirement. The total daily requirement of sodium is   **a)** 1,400   **b)** 2,400   **c)** 3,400   **d)** 4,400   milligrams.

2. Food Label 1 shows that there are 2 g of dietary fiber, which is 8% of one's total daily requirement. The total daily requirement of dietary fiber is   **a)** 5   **b)** 15   **c)** 20   **d)** 25   grams.

Name: _____ Date: _____

FOOD LABELS (cont.)

Food Label Practice

Read the food label and answer the questions that follow.

Food Label 2	Nutrition Facts	2,000-calorie diet
Calories 60	Calories from fat 15	
		% Daily Value
Total fat	1.3 g	2%
Saturated fat	1 g	5%
Trans fat	0 g	
Cholesterol	30 mg	10%
Sodium	432 mg	18%
Total Carbohydrates	< 1 g	0%
Sugar	< 1 g	
Protein	19 g	
Vitamin C		20%

Fill in the blanks with the answers that correctly complete each statement.

1. The total calories are _____.

2. The calories from fat are _____.

3. The amount of fat is _____ grams.

4. The amount of saturated fat is _____ gram.

5. The amount of trans fat is _____ grams.

6. The amount of saturated fat is _____% of

   one's daily requirements for saturated fat.

7. The amount of sodium is _____ mg.

8. The amount of protein is _____ grams.

9. The amount of Vitamin C is _____ percent of daily requirements.

10. The daily requirement of cholesterol is _____ mg.

11. The daily requirement of total fat is _____ g.

Name: _____ Date: _____

  FOOD LABELS (cont.)

Analyzing Food Labels

When you are counting calories and planning a healthy diet, it is important to read food labels. The first thing to note is the number of servings and the number of calories per serving. The fat calories are also important. Note from which type of fat the calories come. Saturated fat comes from animals and dairy products and must be limited in the diet. It is better to have a higher percentage of monounsaturated or polyunsaturated fats, which come from plant sources. Trans fats, which are made by adding hydrogen to vegetable oils, are found in many foods and may increase the levels of LDL cholesterol. Trans fats are used to make foods like cookies, cakes, and pastries last longer on the store shelf. Choose foods that have little or no trans fats. The amounts of salt (sodium) and cholesterol are also important. Choose foods where salt and cholesterol are limited. Also, check the amount of fiber. Most people do not get enough fiber in their diets, so choosing foods with higher amounts of fiber is better.

The food labels below are from a loaf of bread, a package of cookies, and cheese. Refer to the labels below to answer the questions on the next page.

Label 3: Bread	**Label 4: Cookies**	**Label 5: Cheese Cubes**
Serving size: 1 slice	Serving size: 2 cookies	Serving size: 8 pieces
Calories per serving: 90	Calories per serving: 170	Calories per serving: 130
Calories from fat: 10	Calories from fat: 70	Calories from fat: 100
Total fat: 1 g	Total fat: 8 g	Total fat: 11 g
Saturated fat: 0 g	Saturated fat: 4.5 g	Saturated fat: 6 g
Cholesterol: 0 mg	Cholesterol: 0 mg	Cholesterol: 30 mg
Sodium: 170 mg	Sodium: 55 mg	Sodium: 200 mg
Total Carbohydrates: 17 g	Total Carbohydrates: 19 g	Total Carbohydrates: 1 g
Dietary fiber: 2 g	Dietary fiber: 0.5 g	Dietary fiber: 0 g
Sugar: 3 g	Sugar: 11 g	Sugar: 0 g
Protein: 4 g	Protein: 1 g	Protein: 7 g

Name: _____ Date: _____

 FOOD LABELS (cont.)

Analyzing Food Labels (cont.)

Choose the answer that correctly completes each statement.

1. The "g" following a number stands for   a) milligrams.   b) centigrams.   c) grams.

2. The "mg" following the number for sodium and cholesterol stands for   a) milligrams.
   b) centigrams.   c) grams.

3. The recommended 2,400 mg of sodium in a diet is equal to   a) 1.4   b) 2.4   c) 3.4
   d) 4.4   grams.

4. The recommendation for less than 300 mg of cholesterol is equal to less than
   a) $\frac{1}{2}$ b) 1   c) 2   d) 3   gram(s).

5. The total number of calories in four cookies, two slices of bread, and eight cheese cubes
   would be   a) 350.   b) 450.   c) 650.   d) 750.

6. The total grams of saturated fat in four cookies, two slices of bread, and eight cheese cubes
   would be   a) 10.5.   b) 12.   c) 13.5.   d) 15.

7. The total grams of carbohydrates in four cookies, two slices of bread, and eight cubes of
   cheese is   a) 42.   b) 52.   c) 62.   d) 73.

8. A daily recommended diet of 2,000 calories should include 300 grams of carbohydrates.
   The food groups that would provide carbohydrates in the diet are
   a) meats and dairy.   b) fruits and vegetables.

9. Refer to the Recommended Daily Diet on page 30 or 42. The recommended amount of
   saturated fat in the daily diet of 2,000 calories is   a) 10 g.   b) 15 g.   c) 20 g.   d) 25 g.

10. Foods with saturated fat are   a) beef, pork, and cheese.   b) olive oil, peanuts, canola
    oil, and fish.

Name: _____ Date: _____

FOOD LABELS (cont.)

Comparing Food Labels

Label 6 shows the label for a reduced-fat granola bar you intend to eat. Compare the contents on the food label with the Recommended Daily Diet for 2,000 calories per day shown below. Answer the questions that follow.

Recommended Daily Diet:	2000 calories
Total fat: less than	65 g
Saturated fat: less than	20 g
Cholesterol: less than	300 mg
Sodium: less than	2,400 mg
Total Carbohydrates:	300 g
Dietary Fiber:	25 g

Label 6

Nutrition Facts Table

Amount per Serving	Calories: 100	
		% Daily requirement
Total fat	6.5 g	10%
Saturated fat	2 g	10%
Polyunsaturated fat	2 g	
Monounsaturated fat	2.5 g	
Trans fat	0 g	
Cholesterol	0 mg	0%
Sodium	80 mg	30%
Total carbohydrates	21 g	7%
Dietary fiber	11 g	44%
Sugars	10 g	
Protein	4 g	
Vitamin A		25%
Vitamin C		10%
Calcium		15%
Iron		7%
Thiamin		6%
Riboflavin		10%
Niacin		15%
Vitamin B		10%

Name: _____ Date: _____

FOOD LABELS (cont.)

Comparing Food Labels (cont.)

Choose the answer that correctly completes each statement.

1. The total fat in the food in Label 6 is **a)** 2.5 **b)** 4.5 **c)** 6.5 **d)** 8.8 grams.
2. The recommended total fat for the 2,000-calorie diet is **a)** 20 **b)** 45 **c)** 65 **d)** 75 grams.
3. The total saturated fat in the food in Label 6 is **a)** 2 **b)** 4 **c)** 6 **d)** 8 grams.
4. The total cholesterol in the food in Label 6 is **a)** 0 **b)** 1 **c)** 2 **d)** 3 milligrams.
5. The recommended total cholesterol in the 2,000-calorie diet is less than **a)** 100 **b)** 200 **c)** 300 **d)** 400 milligrams per day.
6. The total sodium in the food in Label 6 is **a)** 20 **b)** 40 **c)** 60 **d)** 80 milligrams.
7. The total recommended sodium in the 2,000-calorie diet is less than **a)** 2,400 **b)** 2,600 **c)** 2,800 **d)** 3,000 milligrams per day.

Summary of Labels 3, 4, 5, 6

Today you were hungry. You had three slices of bread from Label 3, six cookies from Label 4, sixteen cubes of cheese from Label 5, and two granola bars from Label 6. Use the Recommended Daily Diet on page 42 and tally up the totals for everything you ate. Be sure to indicate grams (g) or milligrams (mg).

	Bread Label 3	Cookies Label 4	Cheese Label 5	Granola Bar Label 6	Total
Calories					
Total fat					
Saturated fat					
Cholesterol					
Sodium					
Total Carbs.					
Dietary Fiber					

Answer the following for Labels 3, 4, 5, and 6.

8. For which unhealthy nutritional category on the Recommended Daily Diet did you exceed the recommended amount? _____
9. One of the health risks with saturated fat is _____ arteries leading to heart problems.
10. For which healthy nutritional category on the Recommended Daily Diet did you fall far short of eating the recommended daily amount? _____

Name: _____ Date: _____

 # FOOD LABELS (cont.)

Comparing Food Labels (cont.)

You are trying to limit your daily calories to 2,000. It is the end of a long day, and you are too tired to fix a meal at home. You stop by a fast-food restaurant and get a fast-food burger with cheese and a large order of fries. The burger with cheese has 300 calories, 12 g of total fat, 6 g of saturated fat, 0.5 g trans fat, 40 mg of cholesterol, 33 g of carbs, 2 g of fiber, and 750 mg of sodium. The order of fries has 500 calories, 25 g of total fat, 3.5 g of saturated fat, 0 mg of cholesterol, 63 g of carbs, 6 g of fiber, and 350 mg of sodium.

Complete the blanks for your diet for the day. Remember, you have already had the servings of the items from Labels 3, 4, 5, and 6 listed on page 43. Fill in those blanks with the totals from page 43. Be sure to indicate grams (g) or milligrams (mg).

	Snacks from pg. 43	+	Burger with cheese	+	French fries	=	Total for the day
Calories	_____		_____		_____		_____
Total fat	_____		_____		_____		_____
Saturated fat	_____		_____		_____		_____
Cholesterol	_____		_____		_____		_____
Sodium	_____		_____		_____		_____
Total Carbs.	_____		_____		_____		_____
Dietary Fiber	_____		_____		_____		_____

Using the above chart and the Recommended Daily Diet on page 42, choose or fill in the answers that correctly complete each statement.

11. I exceeded the recommended daily diet for calories by a) 40. b) 140. c) 240. d) 340.

12. I know the extra calories will be turned into _____, and I will gain weight.

13. I exceeded the recommended daily diet for total fat of 65 g by a) 34 b) 48 c) 58 d) 64 grams.

14. I exceeded the recommended daily diet for saturated fat of less than 20 g by a) 19 b) 20 c) 21 d) 22 grams.

15. Consuming more fat than is recommended will result in a) weight loss. b) weight gain.

16. I came close to the recommended daily diet of 2,400 mg for a) fiber b) cholesterol c) sodium.

17. Consuming more salt than is recommended may lead to _____ _____ pressure.

18. My diet included less than the recommended daily requirements for which healthy nutritional category? _____

Name: _____ Date: _____

FOOD LABELS (cont.)

Comparing Food Labels (cont.)

Complete the blanks for your diet for the day if you had substituted a salad for the order of french fries and had a burger without cheese. A burger with no cheese has 250 calories, 9 g of total fat, 3.5 g of saturated fat, 25 mg of cholesterol, 520 mg of sodium, 31 g of carbs, and 2 g of fiber. A salad with grilled chicken has 220 calories, 6 g of total fat, 3 g of saturated fat, 75 mg of cholesterol, 890 mg of sodium, 12 g of carbs, and 3 g of fiber.

	Labels 3, 4, 5, 6	+	Burger (no cheese)	+	Salad (with chicken)	=	Total for the day
Calories	_____		_____		_____		_____
Total fat	_____		_____		_____		_____
Saturated fat	_____		_____		_____		_____
Cholesterol	_____		_____		_____		_____
Sodium	_____		_____		_____		_____
Total Carbs.	_____		_____		_____		_____
Dietary Fiber	_____		_____		_____		_____

Using your diet above, complete the following. Place the letter "T" on the blank if the statement is true. Place the letter "F" on the blank if the statement is false. Use the Recommended Daily Diet on page 42.

_____ 19. If I had chosen the plain burger and a salad with chicken, I would be within the daily recommended diet for calories eaten per day.

_____ 20. If I had chosen the plain burger and a salad with chicken, I would have eaten more fat than is recommended per day.

_____ 21. Too much fat in one's diet is a leading cause of weight gain.

_____ 22. If I had chosen the plain burger and a salad with chicken, I would have eaten much more sodium than is recommended per day.

_____ 23. Too much salt in one's diet is a leading cause of high blood pressure.

_____ 24. If I had chosen the plain burger and a salad with chicken, I would have consumed many more carbs than is recommended per day.

_____ 25. If I had chosen the plain burger and a salad with chicken, I would have consumed more fiber than is recommended per day.

_____ 26. If I want to eat a healthy lifestyle diet, I need to cut down on the fat in my diet.

_____ 27. If I want to eat a healthy lifestyle diet, I need to include more fiber in my diet.

_____ 28. If I want more healthy carbs and fiber in my diet, I must eat more fruits and vegetables.

Name: _____ Date: _____

EVALUATING MY LIFESTYLE

Figuring Body Mass Index

The Body Mass Index (BMI) may be used to help you determine if you are overweight. It is a comparison of your weight to a range that is normal for your height. To determine your Body Mass Index, you must first find your height and weight. Find your height in <u>inches</u> and your weight in <u>pounds</u>.

Formula: Weight • 703 ÷ height ÷ height = Body Mass Index

Example: John weighs 140 pounds and is 5 feet 5 inches tall, or 65 inches.

Formula for John's BMI: 140 pounds • 703 = 98,420 ÷ 65 inches = 1,514 ÷ 65 = 23.29, which would round down to 23.

A normal BMI is between 18 and 25. A BMI between 25 and 30 indicates one is overweight. A BMI over 30 is an indication of being obese.

In John's case, his BMI of 23 is in the normal range.

Compute the BMI for the following. Determine if each individual's BMI is normal, overweight, or obese. For #4, compute your own BMI.

1.   Weight 150 pounds, height 60 inches   BMI = _____   _____

2.   Weight 140 pounds, height 50 inches   BMI = _____   _____

3.   Weight 170 pounds, height 70 inches   BMI = _____   _____

4.   Weight _____ pounds, height _____ inches.

     BMI = _____   _____

Name: _____ Date: _____

EVALUATING MY LIFESTYLE (cont.)

Profile for Better Health

1. **My Food Selection Profile:** Carefully choosing the foods that you eat each day will help keep you healthy. Place a plus sign (+) on the blank for those things that guide your selection of foods.

   I check food labels for the amount of:

   _____ a.   fat.

   _____ b.   saturated fat.

   _____ c.   trans fat.

   _____ d.   calories.

   _____ e.   sodium.

   _____ f.   cholesterol.

   _____ g.   sugar.

2. **My Exercise Profile:** Place a plus sign (+) on the blank if the following is true for the exercise you get.

   To improve my physical condition:

   _____ a.   I walk each day.

   _____ b.   I swim each day.

   _____ c.   I jog each day.

   _____ d.   I run each day.

   _____ e.   I take the stairs rather than the elevator.

   _____ g.   I ride a bike each day.

   _____ h.   I am involved in an athletic program.

   _____ i.   I take aerobics classes.

   _____ j.   I _____

   _____

47

Name: _____ Date: _____

EVALUATING MY LIFESTYLE (cont.)

Profile for Better Health (cont.)

3. **My Diet Profile:** Listed below are some of the foods in each food group that make a healthy diet. Place a plus sign (+) on the blank by those foods in each group that you include as part of your diet. There are many other foods that are part of a good diet that could have been included. The purpose of this profile is to help you begin to think about your diet and changes you may need to make. After completing the profile, evaluate: Am I including foods from all four food groups? Am I eating enough whole grains, vegetables, and fruits? How can I improve my diet?

Grains	Meats/Beans/Nuts	Fruits	Vegetables
___ whole-wheat bread	___ black beans	___ apples	___ broccoli
___ wild rice	___ kidney beans	___ strawberries	___ spinach
___ brown rice	___ lean beef	___ blueberries	___ carrots
___ oatmeal	___ eggs	___ oranges	___ sweet potatoes
___ buckwheat	___ catfish	___ bananas	___ asparagus
___ whole-wheat crackers	___ salmon	___ orange juice	___ green beans
___ whole-wheat tortillas	___ chicken	___ peaches	___ potatoes
___ pasta	___ turkey	___ fruit cocktail	___ cucumbers
___ breakfast cereal	___ pinto beans	___ plums	___ lettuce
	___ lean pork	___ raisins	___ brussels sprouts
	___ lean lamb	___ pears	___ tomatoes
	___ soybeans	___ cranberry juice	___ vegetable juice
	___ lima beans	___ grapefruit	___ tomato juice
	___ peanuts	___ melons	___ peppers
	___ trout	___ pumpkin	___ cabbage
	___ herring	___ squash	___ onions
		___ grapes	___ cauliflower
			___ beets
			___ kale
			___ greens

4. If you are eating a healthy diet, most of the servings should come from the fruits and vegetables column. The remaining servings should come from the meat, beans, and nuts column and the grain column.

My BMI, Exercise Profile, and Diet Profile show that to improve my diet for a healthy lifestyle I need to _____

_____

_____

_____

Name: _____ Date: _____

SHAPE UP!

Place a plus (+) beside the things that you would be willing to do to look better, feel better, and have more energy. Put two pluses (++) beside any that you already do.

_____ Walk two miles a day.

_____ Eat at least four fruits and five servings of vegetables every day.

_____ Limit the amount of foods with fat, such as burgers and fries, that I eat.

_____ Eat more whole-wheat pasta, brown rice, and whole-grain cereals.

_____ Use less butter, dressing, and sour cream on salads and potatoes.

_____ Drink more water and limit candy to one bar or less per day.

If you really want to feel better, look better, and have more energy, you must make a conscious decision to do so. You must be willing to make a commitment to accomplish your goal. (If you make a decision to start an exercise program, see your health or physical education teacher for some helpful tips as well as suggestions for a good program.)

Fill in the blanks below with the words listed before each paragraph. A word may be used more than once.

lungs   blood   heart   calories   exercise   200

1. If you are overweight and want to change that, you must reduce the _____ that you consume and develop an exercise program. An exercise program is beneficial because it will increase the efficiency of the _____ and _____. Exercise is also effective in lowering _____ pressure. Although jogging, swimming, or bicycling are great forms of _____, walking is also good _____. Walking at a speed of 3 miles per hour for one hour will burn _____ calories.

appearance   tone   stress

2. Exercise has many benefits besides better health. It can also improve your muscle _____, and that improves your _____. In addition to improving your physical well-being and appearance, exercise reduces _____, improving your emotional well-being, too.

Name: _____ Date: _____

SHAPE UP! (cont.)

routine   20   three   water   exercise   shoes

3. If you are serious about looking better and feeling better, then adequate _____ is important. You must establish a _____ for exercising and maintain it. A good routine includes exercise at least _____ times per week for a minimum of _____ minutes. It is important to have a good pair of _____ that are made for jogging or walking. When exercising, be sure to have plenty of _____ available to drink before and after you exercise.

In addition to how you look and feel, a good diet may prevent many diseases. In the following exercise, complete the blanks with words from the list before each paragraph.

cancer   overweight   blood pressure   35   fat

4. Many health problems are associated with diets that include too much _____. Fat is important in a good diet but should not be more than _____ percent of the calories eaten each day. A diet high in fat is often associated with being _____. A person who is overweight is more likely to have high _____ and some forms of _____.

cancer   intestinal   vegetables   fruits   fiber

5. Fresh _____ and _____ are high in _____. Fiber is important in preventing some forms of _____. A diet high in fiber has an important function in maintaining a healthy _____ tract.

carrots   oranges   grapefruit   Vitamins   sweet potatoes

6. _____ A and C are important in fighting certain diseases. These vitamins are found in vegetables like _____ and _____, and fruits like _____ and _____.

Name: _____   Date: _____

DIET AND EXERCISE: PERSUASIVE LETTER

Write a letter to persuade a friend to team up with you to eat a healthy diet and exercise. In the first paragraph, be specific about the topic you are writing about. In the paragraphs that follow, write about the foods that are part of a healthy diet and what the benefits of the foods are. Use facts and examples of some of the diseases and problems that are likely a result of a poor diet. Include details about the importance of exercise and controlling the number of calories eaten.

Date: _____

Dear _____,

_____

_____

_____

_____

_____

_____

_____

_____

_____

_____

_____

_____

_____

_____

_____

_____

_____

_____

_____

Your friend,

_____

Name: _____ Date: _____

NUTRITIONAL CHOICES: FACE THE CONSEQUENCES

Many times people make poor decisions about what they will eat because they do not have all of the information that they need to make better decisions. People also often ignore the information that they do have. Sometimes people ignore the information and make poor decisions because the consequences seem too far in the future to think about or because the person doesn't believe that he or she will experience the bad consequences.

Our decisions to eat certain foods are often influenced by what our family or friends eat. Often our family or friends don't want to change their diets even if they know that they should. They encourage us to eat a poor diet without even knowing that they are doing it.

In the following exercises, read the decisions and then place the words or phrases listed above each exercise under the appropriate consequence column.

| overweight | loss of energy | poor self-esteem | fatty buildup |
| heart attack | atherosclerosis | stroke/life threatened | loss of lifestyle |

1. Decision Short-term consequence   Long-term consequence   Ultimate consequence

Eat food
high in fat
and salt

_____   _____   _____

_____   _____   _____

_____

- -

more energy	more productive life	better self-concept
longer life	better physical appearance	improved health
less chance for heart attack		atherosclerosis less likely
lower cholesterol levels		lower medical expenses

2. Decision Short-term consequence   Long-term consequence   Ultimate consequence

Have diet
with correct
balance of
protein,
carbo-
hydrates,
and fat.

_____   _____   _____

_____   _____   _____

_____   _____

_____

Eating Disorders: Anorexia and Bulimia

Name: _____ Date: _____

EATING DISORDERS: ANOREXIA AND BULIMIA

Today there is a great deal of media pressure emphasizing thinness. Young people look at the images of thin models, actors, and actresses and begin to feel that is the body type they should have. This media pressure is pointed more toward girls during the high school and college years than it is to boys. However, boys involved in some sports may be pressured into unhealthy eating habits to maintain a certain weight for their sport. The result is that some individuals become overly concerned about weight and appearance. The concern can become so great that dangerous eating habits are developed. Some common characteristics are skipping meals, binge eating and then purging, and over-exercising in an effort to lose more weight. This behavior can result in eating disorders.

Two common eating disorders are anorexia and bulimia. **Anorexia** is an irrational fear of becoming overweight. Someone suffering from anorexia is terrified that they are fat, and they will do anything to lose weight, including exercising for hours and eating nothing for days. Anorexics are essentially starving themselves to death. **Bulimia** is an eating disorder where a sufferer loses control and eats huge amounts of food, sometimes up to 10,000 calories in one sitting. This is called bingeing. But then, out of fear of being fat, they will purge, or throw up, everything they have just eaten and starve themselves until they binge again. Many times, the individual will become compulsive about taking laxative medications. Bulimia destroys a person's stomach, esophagus, and teeth from the stomach acids brought up during purging. Both disorders can lead to muscle weakness and loss, kidney failure, and cardiac arrest.

Place a plus sign (+) on the following statements that are true for you.

_____ 1. I have a fear of becoming overweight.

_____ 2. I often skip meals to make sure that I do not gain weight.

_____ 3. I have family members that have eating disorders.

_____ 4. I often eat large amounts of food and then try to vomit.

_____ 5. My eating behavior and efforts to regurgitate food depress me.

_____ 6. I have sores that do not heal.

_____ 7. I am very tired.

_____ 8. I am constipated and use laxatives frequently.

_____ 9. I exercise more than an hour a day to lose weight.

_____ 10. Some days I need to eat a lot or not at all to maintain a certain weight for my sport.

If you checked three or more statements, you may have a problem. Contact your school counselor, school nurse, or your family doctor for help.

Name: _____ Date: _____

NUTRITION REVIEW CLOZE

Read the following cloze. Complete the blanks using the words in bold.

muscle   fat   meat   weight   proteins   growth   beans

Protein is important in developing and maintaining a healthy cell structure. Protein also forms most of the **1)** _____ in the body. Protein is needed to maintain body tissue and is important in the normal **2)** _____ and development of young people. Although protein is a necessary part of a nutritious diet, when one eats more than is required for a healthy diet, the excess protein is stored as fat. Storage of excess **3)** _____ can result in being overweight. Maintaining the proper **4)** _____ for your height and age is very important in developing a healthy lifestyle. Eating a healthy diet is important in maintaining proper weight.

In planning a diet, it is important to know that proteins can be essential or nonessential. Essential **5)** _____ are known as complete proteins. It is important to choose foods that are sources of essential proteins. Essential protein is found in foods like eggs, meat, milk, cheese, nuts, and **6)** _____. Meat is a good source of essential protein. Excellent meat choices for a healthy lifestyle are fish, chicken without skin, and lean **7)** _____.

ounces   cholesterol   protein

Although meat is a very good source of protein, too much **8)** _____ from meat is detrimental to one's health. The size of meat portions should be approximately three **9)** _____. There are dangers in eating more protein than is required for a healthy lifestyle. Weight gain and increased **10)** _____ levels are only two of the possible undesirable side effects of a diet consisting of too much protein.

bran   heart   grain   germ   wild   carbohydrates

Carbohydrates are a source of energy and provide vitamins, minerals, and fiber in the diet. Fruits, vegetables, and whole grains found in cereals and brown bread are **11)** _____. Bread made from whole grains may range in color from black to brown. Additionally, the texture of whole- **12)** _____ breads is coarser. The dark color and coarse texture of whole-grain breads is because the endosperm,

Name: _____ Date: _____

NUTRITION REVIEW CLOZE (cont.)

13) _____, and germ are retained as part of the bread. White bread is refined, so the bran and 14) _____ have been removed along with many of the vitamins, fiber, and minerals. Those who make whole-grain breads a part of their diet are less likely to be obese or have 15) _____ problems and diabetes. In addition to whole-grain bread and crackers, other whole-grain foods include 16) _____ rice, brown rice, whole wheat, and whole oats.

food   diet   vegetables   cancer   overeat   fiber

Most people do not eat enough healthy carbohydrates and therefore do not get enough minerals, vitamins, and 17) _____ in their diet. Many fruits, vegetables, nuts, beans, and whole grains contain fiber. Although fiber is an important part of a healthy diet, fiber actually has no 18) _____ value. The value of fiber is that it adds bulk to the 19) _____. Fiber is more filling, making it less likely you will 20) _____, and it aids in the passage of food through the intestines. Fiber is thought to be important in the prevention of diseases such as colon 21) _____, diabetes, and heart problems. It is important to remember that fiber is found in nutritious foods such as fruits, 22) _____, nuts, beans, and whole grains.

fruits   diet   fiber

If you have not been getting enough fiber in your diet, you should think about adding more 23) _____ and vegetables to your diet. Those whose diet has not included enough 24) _____ may experience some discomfort when increasing the amount of fiber in the 25) _____. This discomfort usually goes away as your body gets used to the new diet.

energy   animal   blood   cholesterol   room   diabetes

Fats are important sources of 26) _____. Fat in the right amount is an important part of diet. However, eating foods with too much fat can lead to obesity, diseases of the heart, 27) _____, and increased likelihood of some types of cancer. In choosing fats, it is important to know that fats may be saturated or unsaturated. Saturated fats are found in 28) _____ meats and some vegetable oils. Saturated fats are solid

Name: _____ Date: _____

NUTRITION REVIEW CLOZE (cont.)

at **29)** _____ temperature. Unsaturated fats remain liquid at room temperature. It is important to reduce the amount of saturated fat in one's diet. Eating too much saturated fat may cause heart trouble, stroke, and increase the **30)** _____ level in the blood. Excess cholesterol increases the likelihood of high **31)** _____ pressure, resulting in heart problems or stroke.

> **fat   cholesterol   omega-3   polyunsaturated   plant   saturated   limited**

     Because a part of a good diet includes a measured amount of fat, it is important to balance the diet between saturated fats, monounsaturated fats, and polyunsaturated fats. A diet for a healthy lifestyle may include fat from all three of these **32)** _____ sources. The fat from red meat and dairy products is **33)** _____ fat. These fats are solid at room temperature. Because the fats from these sources are likely to increase **34)** _____ levels, a healthy lifestyle diet limits saturated fat to seven percent of the required daily fat intake. Therefore, the amount of fat from these sources should be **35)** _____. A diet for a healthy lifestyle includes an increase in the fat from monounsaturated and **36)** _____ fat sources. Sources of these fats include **37)** _____ oils from sources like olive oil, canola oil, sunflower seeds, soybeans, and peanuts. The fat from eating certain kinds of fish has been found to be very beneficial. Many fish contain **38)** _____ fatty acids, which are good for the heart. A healthy lifestyle diet should include fish on a weekly basis.

> **trans   limited   cholesterol   cookies**

     When hydrogen is added to unsaturated fats, the fats go through a change. The change results in hydrogenated fats, also called trans fats. Trans fats increase the **39)** _____ level, so they must be used sparingly. When purchasing foods, it is important to note on the food label the amount of **40)** _____ fat in the food item. Trans fats are most often found in foods like **41)** _____ and shortenings. Therefore, foods with trans fats such as shortenings and baked goods should be **42)** _____ in the healthy lifestyle diet.

Name: _____ Date: _____

NUTRITION REVIEW CLOZE (cont.)

calories   jellies   diet

Too much sugar in the diet is one of the main sources of obesity. Sugar in the diet contributes a large amount of **43)** _____ but little food value. Candy, soft drinks, jams, **44)** _____, and processed foods are often very high in sugar. Processed foods are high in saturated fat but also high in sugar. Because excess sugar results in increased intake of calories with little food value, in a healthy lifestyle **45)** _____, sugar must be limited.

weight   reduced   calories   fat   sugar   diabetes

To lose **46)** _____, you must reduce your calories. To lose weight, reduce the foods that have high amounts of **47)** _____ and fat. Certainly, this is a positive step toward controlling weight. However, it is the total **48)** _____ consumed that will determine weight loss. Eating low-fat foods may have a positive impact on lowering cholesterol levels, heart problems, and **49)** _____. However, to reduce weight, you must reduce calories. Replacing foods that are loaded with fat calories with foods that have less **50)** _____ and sugar will not result in weight loss if the calories consumed are not **51)** _____.

Starving yourself is not part of a healthy lifestyle. A healthy lifestyle includes a balanced diet that includes protein, carbohydrates, fiber, and fat from foods that are nutritious and healthy. A healthy lifestyle also includes controlling weight gain by not consuming more calories than required on a daily basis.

salt   diet   stroke   bologna   spoiling   high

Excessive salt in the diet is not part of a healthy lifestyle. In earlier times, salt was used to preserve meat and keep it from **52)** _____. This led to Americans having a taste for excessive amounts of **53)** _____ in their diet. To lead a healthy lifestyle, the tendency to use excess amounts of salt must be controlled. The heavy use of salt often leads to **54)** _____ blood pressure. High blood pressure often leads to heart problems and **55)** _____. In addition to limiting the salt added to foods when eating, it is important to become a better grocery shopper. Many cheeses, packaged meats like **56)** _____ and summer sausages, and soups contain large amounts

Name: _____ Date: _____

NUTRITION REVIEW CLOZE (cont.)

of salt. Check the label of canned items and check the salt content. A **57)** _____ for a healthy lifestyle should not include more than 2,400 mg of salt.

> **vegetables   healthy   calories   sugar**

In planning a diet for a healthy lifestyle, eat more fruits, **58)** _____, unsaturated fats, whole grains, and limit the amount of **59)** _____ and salt. One of the benefits of a healthy lifestyle diet is weight control. Eating more **60)** _____ than are burned leads to weight gain. It is important to remember that weight gain is possible on a **61)** _____ lifestyle diet if excess calories are eaten.

> **weight   physical   diseases   exercise**

A healthy lifestyle diet encourages you to eat a balanced diet of foods that are likely to be beneficial in preventing **62)** _____ such as diabetes, heart problems, cancer, and high blood pressure. Maintaining a **63)** _____ that is appropriate for one's age and body type is important. If your weight is above the weight recommended for your age and body type, then you are likely eating portions that are larger than needed, or you are not getting enough **64)** _____. If your weight is below the recommended weight for your age and body build, you may need to increase serving sizes. This may be particularly true for those who are engaged in sports where there is a great emphasis on **65)** _____ activity.

> **energy   blood   cholesterol   diseases**

There are many benefits from eating a healthy lifestyle diet. Immediate benefits include controlling weight, feeling better, and having more **66)** _____. Those who eat a healthy lifestyle diet are less likely to experience heart problems, cancer, and other life threatening **67)** _____ in later life. A healthy lifestyle diet helps lower cholesterol levels and **68)** _____ pressure. Controlling **69)** _____ levels and blood pressure levels makes heart problems and strokes less likely.

Name: _____ Date: _____

NUTRITION REVIEW CLOZE (cont.)

arteries   diastolic   heart   strokes   blood

When the heart beats, blood is pushed through the arteries. Blood is also moving through the **70)** _____ between heart beats when the heart is at rest. If the arteries are blocked, then the heart must pump harder to push the **71)** _____ through the arteries. A blood pressure reading gives two numbers, such as 120/80. The top number, called systolic pressure, is when the **72)** _____ is beating. The bottom number, called **73)** _____ pressure, is when the heart is at rest between beats. The higher the blood pressure numbers, the more difficult it is for blood to move through your arteries and the harder the heart must work. High blood pressure is a primary cause of heart problems and **74)** _____.

fat   deposits   diet   blood   good   cholesterol

Cholesterol is a combination of fat and proteins carried in the blood stream. The small **75)** _____ particles are known as lipoproteins and triglycerides. The **76)** _____ level is checked using a blood test. A small amount of blood is taken to measure the total cholesterol, low-density lipoprotein (LDL), and high-density lipoprotein (HDL) levels. HDL and LDL are both lipoproteins. A high reading for LDL means that fatty **77)** _____ may be building on the walls of the arteries. The fatty deposits will restrict **78)** _____ flow through the arteries, which leads to heart attack or stroke. For this reason LDL is often called the "bad" cholesterol. HDL is often called the **79)** "_____" cholesterol. HDL carries cholesterol away from the arteries to the liver, where it is safely eliminated. A healthy lifestyle **80)** _____ is recommended to lower the LDL cholesterol level and increase the HDL cholesterol level.

glucose   adults   bruises   diabetes

Diabetes is a disease that affects both children and **81)** _____. Today, because so many are overweight and do not eat a healthy lifestyle diet, **82)** _____ has become more common among young people. The test for diabetes is a blood test to check the level of glucose in the blood. A high level of **83)** _____ may indicate a diabetic condition. The symptoms of a possible diabetic condition include frequent thirst, weight loss, tiredness, and slow-healing cuts and **84)** _____.

Name: _____ Date: _____

EXPOSURE TO SUNLIGHT

The Sun: Friend or Foe?

Friend

Sunshine is important because it provides our bodies with vitamin D. If we do not get enough sunlight, a vitamin D deficiency results. Vitamin D helps the body absorb calcium and phosphorus from the foods we eat. It promotes bone formation. Vitamin D benefits our immune system, and it may

be important in limiting some forms of cancer. Vitamin D is important to our health. However, in making sure we get enough vitamin D, we must not overexpose our skin to the sunlight.

Foe

It is important to remember that skin cancer is increasing in the United States. Our skin is a very sensitive organ. Skin cancer is one of the most common types of cancer. Light-skinned people burn more easily when in the sun too long. We must take precautions to protect our skin when we are out in the sunlight for recreation or work.

Many people enjoy lying in the sun to get a tan. Others have to work outside in the sun. People also play sports and engage in other types of recreation in the sun. If the skin is not protected from the harmful rays of the sun, the end result may be damage to the epidermis layer of the skin. The **epidermis** is the outer skin layer. Changes in the epidermis are very visible. Any changes in the epidermis layer must be taken seriously. **Skin cancer** results from changes in the skin cells. The cell changes may take many forms, so it is important to know the signs of different types of skin cancer. The chart on page 61 lists the characteristics of the different types of skin cancer.

Protecting Your Skin

Everyone should protect themselves from the sun's harmful ultraviolet rays when they are outdoors. Wearing sunscreen with a minimum Sun Protection Factor (SPF) of 15, hats, and long sleeves and pants can prevent the sun from damaging the skin. People should avoid lying in the sun or using a tanning bed to get a suntan. Some sun exposure is necessary to have an adequate amount of vitamin D in the body, but you should avoid staying in the sun too long. It is especially important to avoid getting a sunburn.

We need to check our skin for changes that indicate we are developing skin cancer. Each of us can check our bodies for the warning signs of skin cancer. We should check our skin carefully. Look for changes in the shape or size of a mole; scaliness, bleeding, and oozing of a new bump; the pigment spreading from the mole to nearby skin; itchiness; tenderness; and pain.

Periodic visits to a **dermatologist** are also a good idea. These skin doctors are trained to detect skin cancer and treat it. This is particularly important as we become older. However, even young people should have a periodic check if they are out in the sun with their bare skin exposed for long periods of time.

Name: _____ Date: _____

EXPOSURE TO SUNLIGHT (cont.)

Types of Skin Cancers

The following chart lists the different types of skin cancers and the characteristics of each type.

Skin Cancer	Characteristics
Actinic Keratoses A growth on the epidermis skin layer Results from long periods in the sun Precancerous	Skin may become dry and scaly Dark color, such as red or brown Common on the ears, neck, and lips Often itches
Basal Cell Carcinoma Common form of skin cancer Results from long periods in the sun	Bump on skin that grows slowly Bleeding crust Penetrates deep into the skin layers Common on parts of body exposed to 　　long periods of sunlight Red or pink; often a small bump Often appears to heal then come back
Squamous Cell Carcinoma Common skin cancer Results from long periods in the sun Serious	Scaly patch on skin Often red color that grows in size Common on face, ears, neck, and lips May spread to other body parts Asymmetrical in shape
Malignant Melanoma Very serious and deadly skin cancer Results from long periods in the sun 　　and/or severe blistering sunburns 　　early in life Abnormal growth of the pigment- 　　producing cells in the skin that 　　can invade other tissues	Changes in a mole Diameter often larger than $\frac{1}{4}$ inch Scaly with bleeding Painful in the area of the skin cancer Spreads to other body parts May be multicolors of red, blue, black, 　　or brown

Name: _____ Date: _____

EXPOSURE TO SUNLIGHT (cont.)

Sun and Skin Cancer Checklist

Complete the following checklist. Place a check mark on the blanks if the statement is true for you.

_____ 1. I wear a hat when in the sun.

_____ 2. I apply sunscreen with Sun Protection Factor (SPF) of

           15 or better to exposed skin when in the sun.

_____ 3. I apply sunscreen every hour if I'm in the water or perspiring a great deal.

_____ 4. I wear long sleeve shirts to protect my arms from the sun.

_____ 5. I check my body for changes in my skin, moles, etc.

_____ 6. I check all body parts, including the bottoms of my feet.

_____ 7. I limit the periods of time I'm in the sun with my skin exposed.

_____ 8. I do not expose my skin during the middle part of the day when the ultraviolet rays

           from the sun are the strongest.

_____ 9. I know the signs for precancerous growths and skin cancer.

_____ 10. I have periodic checkups by a dermatologist.

List some other things you can do to prevent being overexposed to sunlight and to avoid skin cancer.

_____

_____

_____

_____

_____

_____

Name: _____ Date: _____

LIVING WITH STRESS

De-Stressing

Stress is anything that upsets you or produces anxiety. Stress usually includes nervous feelings and emotional responses. All of us experience stress at times. In fact, some stress is good and increases our effectiveness. When you are asked to make a class presentation, you feel stress. The stress makes you prepare for the presentation because you want to do a good job. When the presentation is over, the stress usually goes away. It is when you experience stress for a long period of time that stress can become harmful.

Stress-producing situations may be physical or emotional. Physical stress might occur when you are working long hours, going to school, and trying to make an athletic team all at the same time. All of the physical activity without enough rest finally wears you out. Emotional stress might occur in a situation where there is a lot of arguing and fighting. Another emotionally stressful situation might occur when you don't complete your homework and feel that you are getting so far behind that your grades are going to suffer.

You may or may not be able to control stress-producing situations. If the stress-producing situation is one that you can control, then you can make a decision to remove the stress. If the stress-producing situation is not under your control, you may not be able to remove that stress-producing situation. However, there are things that you can do to relieve the stress. The following activities may suggest strategies for relieving stress.

Match the stress-causing situations below to their stress-reducing actions. You may use an answer more than once, and some situations may have more than one answer.

_____ 1. homework not complete

_____ 2. friends make decisions for you

_____ 3. grades are low

_____ 4. fear of disease

_____ 5. sick friend

_____ 6. being overweight

_____ 7. you don't make a team

_____ 8. friend driving recklessly

A. plan an exercise schedule and eat properly

B. organize your time, schedule a time to study

C. visit friend, be available to talk and listen

D. find another activity to enjoy or improve your skill

E. seek health official's advice and follow it

F. calmly show disagreement when you need to

G. refuse to ride with person until they drive safely

H. listen, don't accuse, don't make excuses

Name: _____ Date: _____

LIVING WITH STRESS (cont.)

Stress Inventory

Identify the situations below. Place a plus (+) in the blank by any situation that would make you anxious or nervous. Place two pluses (++) in the blank by any situation that would make you extremely anxious or nervous. Place a minus (-) by the situations that would not make you anxious or nervous.

_____ friends arguing	_____ grades
_____ competing in sports	_____ friends ignoring you
_____ not making a team	_____ changing schools
_____ not completing homework	_____ family arguments
_____ being around people that you don't like	_____ loss of a family member
_____ arguing with friends	_____ a sick friend
_____ concern for your physical appearance	_____ problems with the law
_____ fear of catching a disease	_____ loss of a friend
_____ concern for your personal safety	_____ people using alcohol
_____ a sick family member	_____ people using drugs
_____ friends doing something that you don't agree with	_____ bullies
_____ possible pregnancy (you or girlfriend)	_____ friends using drugs
_____ neighborhood problems	_____ moving to a new house

When people experience stress for long periods of time, there are common reactions. The following is a list of some of the signs of stress. Place a plus (+) by those that you have experienced. Place two pluses (++) by any that you have experienced frequently.

_____ extremely nervous	_____ trouble sleeping	_____ irritable
_____ overeating frequently	_____ quick to anger	_____ dizziness
_____ can't sit still	_____ hands tremble	_____ sarcastic
_____ tense a lot	_____ mind wanders	_____ headaches
_____ can't remember things	_____ diarrhea	_____ no energy
_____ crying a lot		

Name: _____ Date: _____

LIVING WITH STRESS (cont.)

You Decide: Stressful Decisions

Situation 1:

Arianna looked at the paper with the word "sloppy" boldly written at the top. Her eyes fell on the sentence written in red along the side of the second paragraph. "I can't read this," it said, "It doesn't make sense." Written at the bottom of the page was a more personal note that said, "Ari, we need to talk. You were a much better student last semester. Is everything O.K.?"

Just then the bell rang and students began to pick up their books and move to their next classes. Arianna hesitated and then bolted for the door. Tears welled up in her eyes as she thought, "If only. . ."

1. In the blanks below, write what you think Arianna's problem might be.

   _____

   _____

2. Is Arianna experiencing stress? If so, is the stress under her control?

   _____

3. Could Arianna do anything more to relieve the stress that she might feel?

   _____

   _____

Situation 2:

Roderick peered around the corner. He couldn't see anyone, but he wasn't sure. Maybe he should have gone another way. He felt his pockets and checked his shoe laces. Any extra bulk or anything that might trip him. . . Wiping his sweaty hands against his jeans, he wondered if he could protect himself. Suddenly he heard someone behind him, and then a voice hissed, "Hey, kid. . ."

1. What do you think Roderick's problem is?

   _____

   _____

2. What could Roderick do to relieve the stress he is feeling?

   _____

   _____

   _____

Name: _____ Date: _____

LIVING WITH STRESS (cont.)

How You Handle Stress

Read each of the pairs of statements below. Place a plus sign (+) on the blank by the statement in each pair that best describes how you often handle stress that occurs with friends or coworkers.

Pair 1

_____ **a.** When I feel offended, I get in the other person's face quickly.

_____ **b.** When I feel offended, I take time to think about how I will respond.

Pair 2

_____ **a.** When I feel offended, it is important to determine who is to blame.

_____ **b.** When I feel offended, it is not so important to determine blame.

Pair 3

_____ **a.** When I feel offended, it is important to state exactly why I feel offended.

_____ **b.** When I feel offended, it is not important to state exactly why I feel offended.

Pair 4

_____ **a.** When I feel offended, I give the other person the time to explain his/her actions.

_____ **b.** When I feel offended, it is important that I state my feelings first.

Pair 5

_____ **a.** When I feel offended, I usually just let it go and try to forget it.

_____ **b.** When I feel offended, I try to let it go, but I cannot forget it.

Pair 6

_____ **a.** When I feel offended, I want to find out what caused the offense.

_____ **b.** When I feel offended, I don't care about what caused the offense.

Pair 7

_____ **a.** I believe most stressful situations can be resolved.

_____ **b.** I do not believe most stressful situations can be resolved.

Pair 8

_____ **a.** I believe stressful situations must be allowed to build like a pyramid until the situation becomes so stressful that all parties will want it resolved.

_____ **b.** I believe letting stressful situations build into a pyramid of stressful situations will be more difficult to resolve.

Name: _____ Date: _____

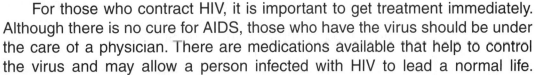

HIV AND AIDS: A FACT OF LIFE

Acquired Immune Deficiency Syndrome (AIDS) is a very serious illness. AIDS is the final stage in a series of illnesses caused by the **Human Immunodeficiency Virus (HIV)**. AIDS weakens the body's natural immune system, making it unable to fight infection. AIDS is spread through contact with bodily fluids. It may be passed from person to person through sexual contact, by sharing needles to inject intravenous drugs, from a mother to her unborn child, through blood transfusions, or through other contact with infected bodily fluids. There is no cure for AIDS, but there are precautions that you can take to keep from contracting HIV.

For those who contract HIV, it is important to get treatment immediately. Although there is no cure for AIDS, those who have the virus should be under the care of a physician. There are medications available that help to control the virus and may allow a person infected with HIV to lead a normal life.

Every human being has an immune system that is designed to protect that person. The **immune system** is prepared to protect the body from infectious agents like viruses, protozoa, bacteria, and fungi. **White blood cells** are the part of the immune system that comes to the rescue when an infectious agent goes into action. These small cells specialize in recognizing the infectious agents that are known as **antigens**. Some of the white blood cells are known as **B-cells**. Their purpose is to produce **antibodies** that attack the antigens that might be harmful to the body.

There are other white blood cells that are called T-cells. T-cells can be helpers or killers. **Helper T-cells** work with the B-cells to make antibodies to fight the antigens. The antibody made is designed to attack the specific infection that is invading the bloodstream. The **killer T-cells** attack the antigens directly.

Antigens have cell walls that are often made from proteins and carbohydrates. These proteins and carbohydrates make up part of the viruses, fungi, bacteria, or protozoa that can be harmful and attempt to destroy the body. When antigens appear in the bloodstream, the B-cells and T-cells spring into action to protect the body.

The immune system is capable of producing different kinds of antibodies to fight the many infections that might invade the body. Typically, when an antigen invades the bloodstream, the B-cells and T-cells are able to destroy the antigen within a seven- to 14-day period. Once the antigen is destroyed and the body is out of danger, some of the B-cells and T-cells have a memory system that protects the body against future invasions of that specific infectious agent.

When the HIV virus enters the bloodstream, it is not recognized as an infectious agent by the immune system. Therefore, the immune system does not spring into action to protect the body as it is designed to do. The body fails to produce the necessary antibodies, and therefore, the HIV virus can continue to develop. The virus then invades the T-cells and begins to reproduce itself.

The HIV virus produces a slow-growing disease that may not produce any signs of illness for months or years. If it is determined that an individual has HIV soon after he or she has contracted the disease and treatment starts immediately, that person may live for many years without developing full-blown AIDS. Treatment for HIV/AIDS involves combining three or more anti-HIV medications in a daily regimen that is sometimes called a "cocktail."

Name: _____ Date: _____

HIV AND AIDS: A FACT OF LIFE (cont.)

Fill in the blanks with the words listed below. A word may be used more than once.

virus(es)	cocktail	antibodies	immune	B	killer
T	white	memory	slowly	many	HIV

The 1) _____ system protects the body from infectious agents like

2) _____, protozoa, bacteria, and fungi. The small, 3) _____ blood cells are

the agents in the 4) _____ system that recognize the infectious agents. The

5) _____ blood cells produce 6) _____ that attack the harmful

infectious agents.

The white blood cells are known as 7) _____-cells and 8) _____-cells. The T-cells

may be helper or 9) _____ T-cells. The helper T-cells and the 10) _____-cells

produce 11) _____ that fight the antigens.

The immune system is capable of producing many different kinds of

12) _____ to fight infections. Typically, the T-cells and B-cells are able to

destroy a 13) _____ in seven to 14 days. The B-cells and T-cells develop a

14) _____ to fight future invasions of the body by that specific infection.

The immune system does not recognize the HIV 15) _____. The immune

system fails to produce the necessary 16) _____ to combat the HIV infection.

The HIV virus grows 17) _____. An infected individual may live for 18) _____

years with the 19) _____ virus. Treatment for HIV/AIDS involves a 20) _____

of three or more anti-HIV medications taken every day.

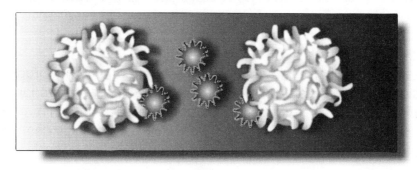

Name: _____ Date: _____

HIV AND AIDS: A FACT OF LIFE (cont.)

Individuals with the HIV virus may appear to be very healthy. In fact, the HIV virus may not test positive for a period of months after contracting the virus. After testing positive for HIV, a person may live a number of years before developing symptoms of the disease AIDS. With medications, a person may live without getting full-blown AIDS for many years.

The scrambled letters on the left can be unscrambled to spell a symptom often associated with the HIV virus or AIDS. Remember, just one or two symptoms does not mean a person has AIDS. Other illnesses, like a cold or the flu, can share these symptoms. But if you engage in risky behavior and have these symptoms, consult your medical professional for testing.

21. EELDBGIN SUGM RO NSEO _____

22. ERFESV FO 100 ROF NTE YADS RO OREM _____

23. GHNIT TSEAWS _____

24. EIGHWT SOLS _____

25. RHEADIAR _____

26. WOLLSEN LYHMP ESNOD _____

27. EAHDHEAC _____

28. RESOS RO HITEW PTOSS NI EHT UOMTH _____

29. EMMRYO ROPBELMS _____

30. Which of the things listed below should you do if you think you or a friend has AIDS? Remember, to make good decisions you must have accurate information. Place a plus sign (+) by each thing listed that would give you more information so that you could make better decisions.

_____ A. Contact the local public health department.
_____ B. Talk to parents.
_____ C. Talk to a counselor.
_____ D. Consult a doctor.
_____ E. Ask your friends if they think you look okay.
_____ F. Contact the state health department.
_____ G. Talk to a friend whose brother is a doctor.

Name: _____ Date: _____

HIV AND AIDS CROSSWORD PUZZLE

Use the clues below to complete the puzzle. You may need to do some research about AIDS to find the answers.

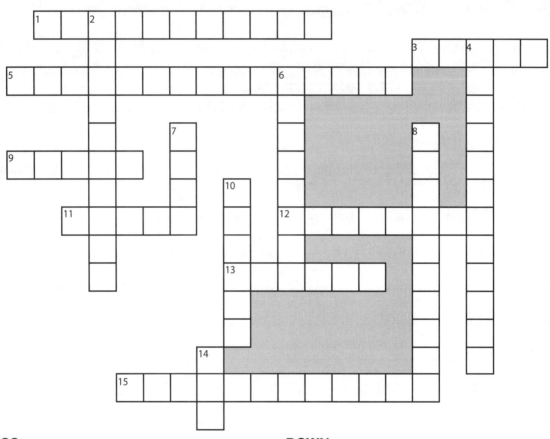

ACROSS

1. While rare today, HIV can be contracted by blood _____.
3. The immune system triggers the production of these blood cells as a defense against infection.
5. The HIV virus attacks these and diminishes the number available to fight infection. (three words)
9. The screening tests for HIV check _____, saliva, or urine for HIV antibodies.
11. Name given to microscopic agent that enters the bloodstream, enters living cells, and causes HIV infection
12. The infectious agents that white blood cells specialize in destroying
13. T-cells may be _____ or killer cells.
15. The HIV virus is transmitted through the exchange of _____ _____.

DOWN

2. Produced by the body's immune system to fight infections
4. The body's natural defense to fight infections (two words)
6. Combination of three or more anti-HIV medications
7. Acronym for Aquired Immune Deficiency Syndrome
8. The immune system protects the body against _____.
10. HIV may be passed from an infected _____ to her unborn child, by sharing infected needles, and through sexual contact.
14. The virus that causes AIDS

Name: _____ Date: _____

HIV AND AIDS: FACT OR FICTION?

1. Place a plus (+) in the blank before each of the words or phrases below if you think that the HIV virus could be contracted in that way.

   _____ sharing food   _____ to the unborn child through its mother
   _____ shaking hands   _____ wearing others' clothes
   _____ sexual intercourse   _____ sitting next to an infected person
   _____ swimming   _____ spending time with an infected person
   _____ using public bathrooms   _____ urine
   _____ blood transfusion   _____ sharing syringes (needles)
   _____ kissing   _____ sweat

2. List the four items above that are most likely to involve the exchange of body fluids (blood and semen) between individuals.

   _____

   _____

   Even though HIV may be contracted through a blood transfusion, there is little chance that this will happen today. All blood donors are tested for the HIV virus. Any individual that is HIV-positive is not allowed to donate blood.

3. The remaining items in the list above are known as casual contact. A person is not likely to contract HIV through such contact. List five of the items that would be considered casual contact.

   _____

   _____

   As you have found in the exercises and in your class discussion, the HIV virus is passed from one individual to another through the exchange of body fluids. Abstinence from using drugs and having sexual intercourse are the best ways to greatly reduce your chances of contracting the HIV virus.

   Today, there are families in which an individual may have the HIV virus. When living in a family situation, there is close contact among members, and precautions should be taken. Keep body fluid contact to a minimum. Maintain a strict level of hygiene and do not share personal items. When in contact with blood, use latex gloves. Wash your hands immediately after taking the gloves off, and dispose of the gloves properly.

   Ask your teacher for more information about HIV and AIDS, and contact your health care provider or local or state health department for more information.

Name: _____ Date: _____

SEXUALLY TRANSMITTED DISEASES

Understanding Sexually Transmitted Diseases

An important part of a healthy lifestyle is being aware of diseases that are transmitted sexually. Many people are unaware of these diseases. Many are under the false impression that sexually transmitted diseases are only found in certain groups of people. This is untrue. Sexually transmitted diseases are found in people from all walks of life. It is true that certain lifestyles make sexually transmitted diseases more likely. If someone contracts a sexually transmitted disease, they must seek medical attention.

Genital Herpes

Genital herpes is one of the most common sexually transmitted diseases. One of the signs of genital herpes is blisters or sores on the genitals. The virus that causes genital herpes may not be obvious for months. Then blisters or sores may appear for a period of time and then appear to heal. However, the disease has not gone away, because the virus that causes genital herpes remains in the carrier's system. Pregnant women who have genital herpes must take special precautions. During birth, genital herpes can be passed to the infant, causing brain damage, blindness, or possibly death. When a woman is pregnant, it is important that she makes the doctor aware that she has the genital herpes virus.

Genital Warts

Genital warts are a sexually transmitted disease. The virus that produces the warts may appear periodically over the person's lifetime. A large number of people carry the virus for genital warts. Those who contract the virus may also be prone to developing certain types of cancer.

Chlamydia

Those who have contracted chlamydia bacteria are often unaware that they have a disease. In some cases, those infected may have a discharge during urination. Left untreated, this sexually transmitted disease can cause inflammation of the pelvic area. In many cases, chlamydia leads to infertility. Babies born to infected mothers are in particular danger of infections.

Hepatitis

Hepatitis is a virus that spreads just like HIV does—through unprotected sexual contact as well as sharing dirty needles and from mother to unborn child. Hepatitis has three main forms: Hepatitis A, Hepatitis B, and Hepatitis C. All forms of hepatitis can attack the liver, leaving sufferers with jaundiced, or yellowed, skin as well as other symptoms, such as abdominal pain, fever and chills, and extreme fatigue. Vaccines for hepatitis exist, so make sure your records are up to date.

Name: _____ Date: _____

SEXUALLY TRANSMITTED DISEASES (cont.)

Understanding Sexually Transmitted Diseases (cont.)

Gonorrhea

Gonorrhea is a sexually transmitted disease caused by a bacteria and characterized by a white or yellow discharge when urinating. Those who contract the disease often experience pain when urinating. Infections of the urinary tract are also common with this disease. Medical treatment is necessary since gonorrhea can cause serious illnesses. Women may experience chronic pelvic pain, and the infection may cause infertility. The disease can spread to the skin and joints and can affect the heart and brain if not treated.

Syphilis

Syphilis is caused by a microorganism spread through sexual contact. A person with syphilis may carry the disease undetected for years. Many years after contracting the disease, the person may experience serious medical problems. Initially, skin ulcers may appear. The disease may be treated with penicillin or other antibiotics, but if left untreated, the infection can damage almost any tissue in the body. The neurological system is particularly vulnerable to syphilis infection. An untreated infection can cause life-threatening damage to the heart, brain, and other organs, leading to blindness, mental illness, and death.

Place a plus sign (+) on the blank by the statement with which you agree.

_____ 1. Sexually transmitted diseases affect many people.

_____ 2. Sexually transmitted diseases do not affect many people.

_____ 3. Sexually transmitted diseases can be prevented.

_____ 4. Sexually transmitted diseases cannot be prevented.

_____ 5. Sexually transmitted diseases are not dangerous

_____ 6. Sexually transmitted diseases are dangerous.

_____ 7. Those with sexually transmitted diseases should receive medical treatment.

_____ 8. Those with sexually transmitted diseases do not need to receive medical treatment.

_____ 9. If I have had a sexually transmitted disease, it is important that I inform my doctor.

_____ 10. If I have had a sexually transmitted disease, it is not important that I inform my doctor.

Name: _____ Date: _____

DRUG USE: WHY RISK IT?

Drugs are widely available and sometimes provide a great temptation to people. **Illegal drugs** are those that the government prohibits the manufacture, sale, purchase, and use of. **Legal drugs** are those that are not prohibited by law from being manufactured, sold, purchased, or used. (Some legal drugs may be limited in their uses and/or distributors, such as prescription drugs. These may also be considered illegal if they are misused.)

The misuse of drugs poses great threats to the health of individuals who use them. Anyone who misuses drugs is also breaking the law and can be jailed if caught. Drug abuse is not limited to illegal drugs. Legal drugs are also abused when individuals use them in an unprescribed way or in quantities exceeding the amount that is recommended. Abusing any drug, legal or illegal, can destroy your health and life.

Illegal drugs

Marijuana is derived from the hemp plant and is known as cannabis. The use of marijuana creates feelings of relaxation and euphoria. Marijuana causes a rapid increase in the pulse rate and is quickly absorbed into the bloodstream, liver, and lungs. Since one marijuana cigarette may be equal to four tobacco cigarettes, marijuana use is very damaging to the lungs and may impair the immune system. The prolonged use of marijuana may cause brain damage with effects similar to those of aging. Young people are particularly affected by the use of marijuana, and often those who use it experience mood changes, loss of ambition, apathy, difficulty in carrying out long-term plans, and decline in school performance or work. Since the use of marijuana impairs the user's judgment and motor skills, it makes driving a car very dangerous.

Cocaine use causes a dilation of pupils, increases the heart rate, and increases the body temperature. The cocaine user experiences feelings of restlessness and anxiety, an inability to sleep, and a loss of the sense of smell. Those who use a needle to inject cocaine directly into their bloodstreams run the risk of contracting AIDS. The use of cocaine increases the risk of emphysema and heart attack. Cocaine users often experience seizures, cardiac arrest, respiratory arrest, or stroke, all of which can lead to death. The use of cocaine is very dangerous since it acts on the pleasure centers of the brain and produces an internal craving for the drug that in turn creates an **addiction**.

Crack cocaine is a cheap form of cocaine that is smoked. In addition to all the risks cocaine has, smoking it in crack form can kill by causing **asphyxia**, where the cells in the body cannot absorb oxygen.

Hallucinogens such as LSD are drugs that create sensations that one can "hear colors" or "see sounds." Hallucinogens may create a sense of overwhelming fear or insanity. The use of hallucinogens increases the heart rate and blood pressure, dilates the pupils, and causes a loss of appetite as well as sleeplessness and restlessness. Those who use these drugs experience impaired mental functioning, decreased attention span, and problems with abstract thinking.

DRUG USE: WHY RISK IT? (cont.)

Opiate drugs include **heroin**. Those who use heroin become easily addicted and have a persistent craving for the drug. The drug causes shallow breathing, nausea, panic, insomnia, convulsions, an elevated pulse rate, and an increase in the body temperature. Since the drug is often injected by needle, the risk of HIV infection is high. The chances of an overdose and death are common.

Methamphetamine, or meth, acts as a powerful stimulant to the body. On the streets, methamphetamines are known as crystal meth when swallowed or as speed and ice when

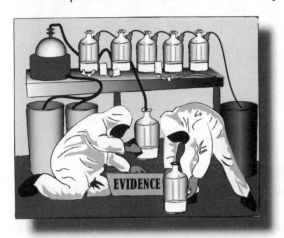

smoked. All meth is dangerous. Users experience paranoia, hallucinations, and violent or erratic behavior. In addition to these mental problems, abusers suffer from dangerous weight loss, open sores on the skin, and the chemicals in meth eat away the enamel on teeth. Meth kills through kidney failure, lung and liver damage, and irreversible brain damage. In addition, the process of making meth is dangerous. The chemicals used are toxic to people, animals, and the environment. Meth labs can frequently explode and cause fires.

Sniffing or **huffing** inhalants can lead to immediate death from cardiac arrest, suffocation, or asphyxia the very first time. **Inhalants** are any group of chemicals that give off toxic fumes that people inhale to get high. Other side effects include headaches that occur within moments, vomiting, rashes around the nose and mouth, and kidney and liver failure.

Ecstasy is a popular designer drug that people take to stay awake at raves. Many people see it as harmless, but ecstasy can cause brain damage, anxiety, and depression, and can lead to heat stroke. The ecstasy that is distributed at parties often has other toxic chemicals mixed in that can have lethal interactions in the body.

Legal drugs

Abusing legal prescription drugs is no safer. Just because a drug is prescribed by a doctor doesn't mean it is a 'safe' high. Using drugs for anything other than their prescribed reasons can lead to addiction, depression, paranoia, or even heart failure.

Painkillers, like OxyContin and Vicodin, and **sedatives**, like Xanax and Valium, are prescribed to adults who store them in medicine cabinets where children can reach them. These drugs can lead to addiction and severe withdrawal symptoms.

Ritalin and other ADD/ADHD drugs are poplar today because students believe these drugs can help them stay awake longer and focus better, leading to higher grades. But unless you are under a doctor's care and the dosage is carefully monitored, you can suffer cardiac arrhythmia, an irregular heartbeat that can cause the heart to stop beating.

Steroids have recently become a problem for younger students. Boys in particular take steroids to bulk up or gain a competitive advantage at sports. Steroids are hormonal substances

DRUG USE: WHY RISK IT? (cont.)

related to testosterone that promotes muscle growth. While steroid users may gain muscle mass, they lose much more. In boys, prolonged steroid use can result in shrunken testicles, impotence, and breast enlargement (called gynecomastia). In girls, steroids can lead to smaller breasts, deeper voices, and more body and facial hair. In both boys and girls, steroids can lead to fatal liver problems, heart disease, and all-over acne. Steroids may also make abusers more violently aggressive, leading to crime sprees and jail time.

While drug use is dangerous for anyone, it is especially harmful for pregnant women to abuse drugs because the drugs can also affect the unborn child. Pregnant women who use marijuana may have premature babies with low birth weights and small heads. Babies born to mothers who abuse drugs often have severe visual, motor, and auditory problems. These babies may also exhibit outbursts and become agitated very easily. Babies of mothers who are heroin users are born addicted to heroin and must go through withdrawal. The babies may also have developmental problems.

When individuals decide to use or not use drugs, they are making a decision that will affect the rest of their lives. Such an important decision may need to be made only once. However, one may need to make the decision many times through one's life, as situations arise. Decisions are always followed by consequences. In making decisions, it is important to have as much information as possible so that you can evaluate the risks. Remember, the misuse and abuse of drugs destroys people's lives, families, and friends.

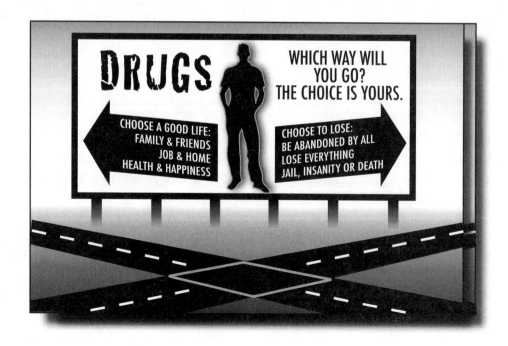

Name: _____ Date: _____

OH, WHAT A TANGLED WEB

A word web helps you to relate everything in a selection that you have read. Complete the following word web by using the words below. Key parts have been completed to get you started. You may use the words more than once.

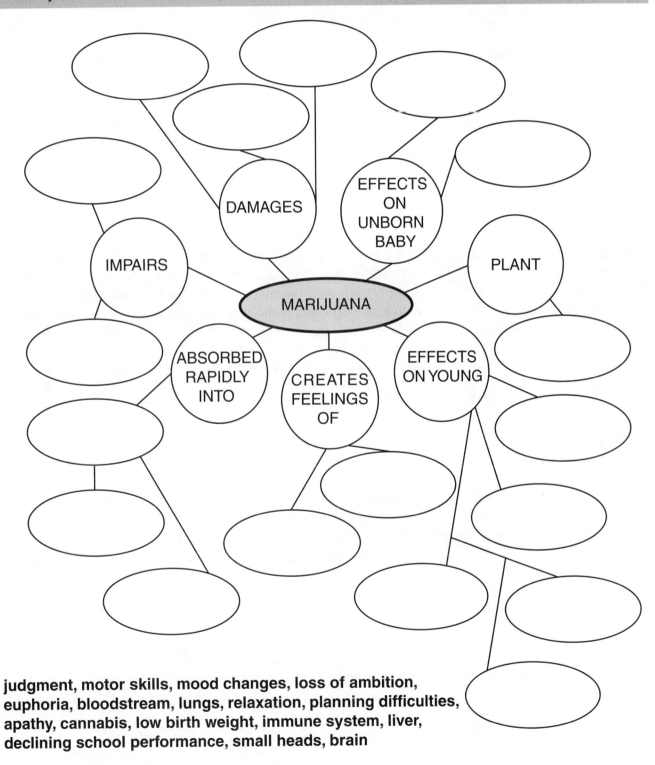

judgment, motor skills, mood changes, loss of ambition, euphoria, bloodstream, lungs, relaxation, planning difficulties, apathy, cannabis, low birth weight, immune system, liver, declining school performance, small heads, brain

Name: _____ Date: _____

DRUG USE: FACE THE CONSEQUENCES

1. There are many consequences of misusing drugs. There are immediate consequences, health risks, and legal consequences. In the exercise below are consequence columns with blanks below each type of consequence. List as many consequences as you can think of for each.

Consequences

immediate	health risks	legal
_____	_____	_____
_____	_____	_____
_____	_____	_____
_____	_____	_____
_____	_____	_____

2. Now review the text on pages 74–76. Can you think of any more consequences? Add these to the bottom of your list. Write any consequences that apply to more than one drug below, and list the drugs that apply to that consequence (whether they are listed on pages 74–76, have been discussed in class, or have been studied by you either on your own or in another class).

    _____

    _____

    _____

    _____

3. Can you think of any positive consequences of misusing drugs? If you can, list them and explain why you think that the consequence would be good. Are any of these consequences long term? Are they lasting, or do they only last as long as the drug is in your bloodstream? Do you think that the positive consequences of misusing drugs outweigh the bad ones listed above? If so, explain.

    _____

    _____

    _____

    _____

    _____

Name: _____ Date: _____

DRUG USE: CROSSWORD PUZZLE

Use the clues below to complete the puzzle. You may have to do some research about drugs to find the answers.

ACROSS
1. A feeling of great happiness or well-being produced by many drugs for a short time
5. Drug whose manufacture, sale, purchase, and use are prohibited by law
10. Drugs that treat stress and tension, such as Valium
12. An internal craving for a drug that leads to compulsive drug use
13. Designer drug often distributed at parties
14. Drug made from opium
15. Chemicals that give off toxic fumes that people huff to get high

DOWN
2. Drugs that create sensations of hearing colors and seeing sounds
3. Drugs that lead to muscle gain and liver cancer
4. Condition that causes death because the body's cells cannot absorb oxygen
6. Drug whose manufacture, sale, purchase, and use are not prohibited by law
7. Drug that is derived from the hemp plant
8. A written order from a doctor describing how to take a legal drug
9. One of the street names of methamphetamines (two words)
11. Virus that can be transmitted through sharing syringes to inject intravenous drugs

Name: _____ Date: _____

DRUG USE: SIGNS OF DEPENDENCE

Those who use drugs and are dependent on drugs often exhibit certain characteristics. In the following exercise, place a plus (+) beside an item if you know someone whose lifestyle has changed to include that characteristic.

_____ misses school more often than he or she used to
_____ less concerned with clothes and general appearance
_____ late for work more often
_____ frequently stays away from school or work due to illness
_____ less friendly toward others
_____ grades in school have dropped
_____ often gets into arguments or fights with others
_____ less energetic, listless, and apathetic
_____ fights with family more
_____ often late for school, meetings, and other events
_____ uses more than a prescribed amount of a legal drug
_____ uses a drug (legal or illegal) all the time
_____ uses several different drugs (legal or illegal) at the same time, in a way other than what a physician prescribed

1. In the exercise above you have information available—the actions of people around you. The exercise above lists several characteristics of the use of and/or dependence on drugs. List the characteristics from above that would lead you to suspect that an individual is abusing drugs. Write those characteristics on the blanks below.

_____

_____

_____

2. List the characteristics that would lead you to the decision that an individual <u>might</u> be on drugs.

_____

_____

_____

_____

_____

Name: _____ Date: _____

IT'S NO JOKE TO SMOKE

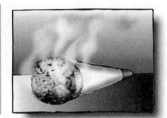

Individuals have reasons for making decisions that affect their lives. There are reasons why individuals make decisions to use or not to use tobacco and tobacco products. Complete the following statements with the first thought that occurs to you. You may want to discuss your answers when you are finished.

I believe that smoking is _____

_____.

Smokers are _____

_____.

Smoking is _____

_____.

If everyone smoked, _____

_____.

If no one smoked, _____

_____.

Smoking improves _____

_____.

Smokers' teeth _____

_____.

Smokers' breath _____

_____.

Smokers' clothes _____

_____.

If I smoke, it is because _____

_____.

Name: _____ Date: _____

AND I'LL HUFF AND I'LL PUFF...

Look for images of people smoking cigarettes or using smokeless tobacco in movies or television shows. Choose the phrases from the list below that best describe the positive images of using tobacco. Write these phrases in the blanks on the left. Write the phrases that describe the negative images of using tobacco in the blanks on the right.

- people enjoying outdoor activities
- people being told they have bad breath
- people inhaling and coughing
- people with wrinkled skin
- people clean and neatly dressed
- people laughing
- people who look physically strong
- people being told that their clothes smell
- people who enjoy life

- people having fun
- discolored teeth
- unhealthy lungs
- babies sick from smoke
- healthy people
- people smiling and happy
- people discussing nicotine
- people who are young
- people who are attractive

Positive Images of Tobacco Use

_____

_____

_____

_____

_____

_____

_____

_____

_____

_____

_____

Negative Images of Tobacco Use

_____

_____

_____

_____

_____

_____

_____

_____

_____

_____

_____

Name: _____ Date: _____

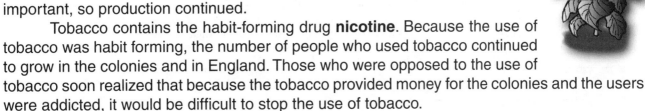

TO SMOKE OR NOT TO SMOKE

The decision to smoke or not should be made in the same way that other decisions should be made. First, it is important to get information that is accurate. Second, the consequences of the decision should be considered.

Tobacco is a weed that was first discovered in the West Indies by the Spanish explorers. When the Europeans settled the American colonies, tobacco became a crop that could be raised in America and sold in London to pay for the supplies needed in the colonies. Many people in the colonies and in England were against the raising of tobacco. They said that smoking was a dirty habit and that the tobacco plant ruined the soil. But the need for a cash crop was important, so production continued.

Tobacco contains the habit-forming drug **nicotine**. Because the use of tobacco was habit forming, the number of people who used tobacco continued to grow in the colonies and in England. Those who were opposed to the use of tobacco soon realized that because the tobacco provided money for the colonies and the users were addicted, it would be difficult to stop the use of tobacco.

Finally, some people began to suspect that tobacco was harmful to the health of those who used it. However, it was some time before the medical community could verify that certain diseases were associated with the use of tobacco. It is now known that the nicotine in tobacco acts as a stimulant, increasing blood pressure and the heart rate. Diseases of the lungs, heart, and kidneys are common among those who have smoked for years. Smokers often develop

cancer, emphysema, and arteriosclerosis. **Arteriosclerosis** is a thickening or hardening of the arteries. **Atherosclerosis** is a particular kind of arteriosclerosis where fatty deposits build up in the arteries and may block blood flow. A heart attack is caused when arteries to the heart are blocked. A stroke occurs after fatty deposits close an artery supplying blood to the brain. Atherosclerosis may begin when damage is caused to the inner layer of an artery by an irritant such as nicotine.

Research has shown that family members who live in homes where there are smokers have many health problems. Children who live in homes where a parent smokes have health problems more frequently than children whose parents do not smoke. The children whose parents are smokers often have more colds, bronchitis, pneumonia, coughs, asthma, ear infections, and lung problems. Women who are nonsmokers who are married to husbands who smoke are more likely to develop lung cancer than nonsmoking women whose husbands do not smoke.

In addition to health risks from the tobacco itself, harmful chemicals may find their way into tobacco products. Since tobacco is a plant that rapidly depletes the soil of its nutrients, the crop must be heavily fertilized. To protect the plants from disease and insects, pesticides that have been proven to cause disease and death in animals and humans are used on them. Many of these chemicals are found in the tobacco that is used to make cigarettes. Those who use tobacco are actually ingesting quantities of these deadly chemicals.

Name: _____ Date: _____

TO SMOKE OR NOT TO SMOKE (cont.)

In the following exercise, read the statement and then answer the questions.

1. It is estimated that 80 percent of those who smoke would like to quit. In your opinion, why don't they?

   _____

   _____

   _____

2. Why do you think that tobacco companies add menthol to cigarettes?

   _____

   _____

   _____

3. If an individual started smoking at the age of 16 and smoked two packages a day at a cost of $4.00 a pack, how much will the tobacco cost each week? Each month? Each year? Over a 40-year period, provided no prices go up and the smoker continues to smoke only two packs per day?

   _____

   _____

4. Can you think of any ways that you would prefer to spend this money if it were yours? If so, list a few.

   _____

   _____

True/False:

_____ 5. People who smoke usually have more wrinkled skin.

_____ 6. People who smoke live longer.

_____ 7. Tobacco contains many harmful chemicals.

_____ 8. Those who advertise tobacco always smoke.

Name: _____ Date: _____

EXPLORING ALCOHOL MYTHS

There are many myths about alcohol. The decisions that individuals make about the use of alcohol must be made with accurate information. The decision to use alcohol is a high-risk decision. Do you have the information that you need to make good choices concerning alcohol? In the following exercise, place a plus (+) by the statements that you believe are true. Place a minus (-) by those that you think are false.

_____ 1. Drinking is a sign that a person has reached adulthood and maturity.

_____ 2. Alcohol contains lots of calories that are converted to fat.

_____ 3. Beer has several nutrients in it.

_____ 4. Alcoholics are weak people who do not want to quit drinking.

_____ 5. When an individual begins drinking as a teenager, he or she is more likely to become an alcoholic.

_____ 6. Drinking alcohol in cold weather will keep you warmer.

_____ 7. Alcohol relaxes the user and lowers his or her inhibitions.

_____ 8. The more often a person drinks, the more likely he or she is to build up an increased tolerance for alcohol.

_____ 9. When people are intoxicated, they reveal their true personalities.

_____ 10. Alcoholics can learn to drink socially without becoming intoxicated.

_____ 11. A cold shower will sober an intoxicated person.

_____ 12. Black coffee will sober an intoxicated person.

_____ 13. Women usually become intoxicated more easily than men.

_____ 14. Pregnant women can drink safely if they are careful.

_____ 15. Alcohol is a drug.

_____ 16. The sons of alcoholics are more likely to become alcoholics if they begin drinking.

_____ 17. Alcohol is not absorbed into the bloodstream as quickly when the stomach is full.

_____ 18. An individual who drinks two drinks per day may be dependent on alcohol.

_____ 19. The liver will only absorb $\frac{1}{2}$ ounce of alcohol per hour.

_____ 20. Alcoholism is a disease.

_____ 21. The use of alcohol will make a person live longer.

_____ 22. The use of alcohol may be damaging to the liver, stomach, and pancreas.

_____ 23. People who start drinking at an older age never become alcoholic.

_____ 24. An intoxicated person will become sober faster if he or she exercises.

_____ 25. Approximately half of the accidental deaths, suicides, and homicides involve individuals who are drinking or drunk.

_____ 26. You should never take medication (including pain medication) with alcohol.

_____ 27. The alcohol in whiskey or gin is stronger than the alcohol in beer.

_____ 28. When a pregnant woman drinks, none of the alcohol affects the baby.

_____ 29. Alcohol is one of the most widely used drugs in the United States.

_____ 30. Alcohol is one of the most widely abused drugs in the United States.

Name: _____ Date: _____

THINK BEFORE YOU DRINK

Alcohol is produced by the fermentation of sugars in cereals and fruits such as barley and grapes. Alcohol has seven calories per gram—three more than carbohydrates and protein. The calories contained in alcohol will change to fat, but there are no vitamins, minerals, or proteins in alcohol. In fact, the use of alcohol depletes the body of many of the important B vitamins. If alcohol is taken in large enough quantities, it is lethal (deadly).

Alcohol acts as a **depressant** on the central nervous system, much like a sedative or tranquilizer. It relaxes the user and reduces his or her inhibitions. Alcohol may impair speech and muscle coordination. It affects the areas of the brain related to thought, emotion, and judgment. Alcohol abuse and alcoholism are major problems associated with the use of alcohol, and they may cause the loss of a person's job, family, or even his or her life. The alcoholic or alcohol abuser often misses work, has been fired from jobs, has family problems or is divorced, has impaired health due to alcohol, and has been arrested for driving while intoxicated. It is estimated that the use of alcohol is involved in over one-half of the accidental deaths, suicides, and homicides in the United States.

The tendency to become alcoholic has both hereditary and environmental components. There is evidence that if the sons of alcoholics drink alcohol, they are more likely to become alcoholics than others. There is also evidence that those who are raised in a home where alcohol is abused are more likely to abuse alcohol or become alcoholics if they begin using alcohol.

A person becomes an **alcoholic** by developing an increased tolerance for the amount of alcohol that he or she can consume. The physical problems resulting from alcoholism include headaches, anxiety, insomnia, nausea, tremors, delirium, and seizures. Drinking more alcohol may relieve the symptoms temporarily, but drinking too much alcohol can lead to alcohol poisoning and even death. Alcoholism is usually associated with health problems such as diseases of the liver, stomach, pancreas, larynx, and esophagus. All of these diseases are common among those who abuse alcohol.

The number of calories an alcoholic drink contains can be figured by a formula. The formula is:

number of ounces of alcohol in a drink X proof of the liquor X 0.8 = number of calories

The proof of alcohol is used to indicate the percent of alcohol. The proof is twice the percentage of alcohol in a liquor. If a liquor is 80 proof, divide 80 by 2 to find the percentage of alcohol in it. An 80 proof liquor is 40 percent alcohol. If the percent of alcohol is known, then the proof can be found by multiplying the percentage of alcohol by two. If a brand of wine is 10 percent alcohol, it is 20 proof.

Name: _____ Date: _____

THINK BEFORE YOU DRINK (cont.)

Use the information on the previous page to solve the problems below.

1. A glass of wine contains 5 ounces. The wine is 10 percent alcohol. What is the proof? How many calories does this glass of wine contain?

   _____

2. A 12-ounce can of beer is five percent alcohol. What is its proof? How many calories are in the can of beer?

   _____

3. A 1 ½-ounce drink of whiskey is poured from a bottle that is 80 proof. What is the percentage of alcohol in this drink? How many calories are in this drink?

   _____

In the following exercise, you will learn the meaning of some terms that are used when talking about alcohol. Each of the following words can be made from the scrambled letters at the beginning of the sentence.

_____ 4. erftaiomnetn: The process by which ethyl alcohol is formed from the sugar in grains like barley or fruits like grapes

_____ 5. biinhinoit: Control over the mental processes that restrain actions and thoughts

_____ 6. cohalol: A colorless, intoxicating agent found in fermented liquors

_____ 7. oprof: Twice the percentage of alcohol in a liquor

_____ 8. oxtniciaetd: The condition of a person who has consumed enough alcohol to be drunk

_____ 9. resedspatn: Alcohol is described in this way because it acts like a sedative or tranquilizer on the central nervous system.

_____ 10. desavtei: Alcohol is described in this way because it may lessen the tendency of a person to become excited or anxious.

_____ 11. iqtrnailrezu: A drug that acts as a depressant on the central nervous system

_____ 12. locachiol: A person who has become dependent on alcohol

Name: _____ Date: _____

 # IT'S UP TO YOU: FETAL ALCOHOL SYNDROME

Many babies are born with defects that are the result of the mother drinking alcohol while she was pregnant. Beer, wine, whiskey, gin, vodka, and other alcoholic beverages are dangerous to a fetus. Two very serious defects are fetal alcohol syndrome (FAS) and fetal alcohol effect (FAE). Children who are born with FAS or FAE may have both physical and mental problems. Physical defects include small birth weight, small head size, heart defects, and growth problems. Mental defects include retardation, nervousness, restlessness, behavior problems, and problems with learning.

Situation:

You have a family member who is pregnant. The woman is of legal drinking age and has been invited to a party. It is likely that alcohol will be available at the party. The family member knows that alcohol is dangerous for a fetus and has not been drinking. If she goes to the party, she will be encouraged to drink. Those who will be encouraging her are people that she considers good friends. Do you think that you should discuss this with the family member?

Even though we cannot assume the responsibility for other people's actions, we do have the responsibility to try to prevent them from making decisions that are high-risk for themselves or others. Blaming, criticizing, or becoming angry won't help. Try to structure your approach so that you have factual information. Remember that you must be a good listener. However, you cannot support such arguments as "Just this once won't hurt" or "I've been under a lot of pressure."

1. How would you approach the family member?

   _____

   _____

2. What information would you present?

   _____

   _____

3. What would you suggest as alternatives to going to the party?

   _____

   _____

4. What would you suggest if the person insisted on going to the party?

   _____

   _____

Name: _____ Date: _____

IT'S UP TO YOU: ALCOHOL AND FRIENDS

Alcohol begins to affect a person with the first drink. Even though every person is affected by alcohol, it affects everyone differently. Alcohol changes the physical and mental state of those who drink. This presents a high risk for those who operate any kind of machinery. It is a very serious problem for those who are old enough to drive a car. Each year, thousands of individuals who have been drinking are involved in serious accidents. You will come in contact with individuals who use alcohol. This means that you will be placed in situations where you must make decisions about such things as whether or not to use alcohol illegally (under age) and whether or not to ride with those who are drinking and driving.

Situation:

You are attending a school party with friends. There is no liquor at the party. When it is time to leave, one of your friends offers you a ride home in his car. When you get to the car, your friend opens the trunk, and you see that there are cans of beer in it. He tells you that his brother, who is of legal age, purchased the beer for him. Your friend says he has enough beer for everyone and offers beer to you and some of your other friends who are there.

Place a plus (+) beside the following statement that is most similar to what you would do.

_____ Wait to see what your other friends are going to do and then make the same decision that they do.

_____ Tell your friend that you will find another way home.

_____ Decide to ride with your friend no matter what decision your friends make.

_____ Tell your friend that you will find another way home, and encourage him not to drink the beer.

_____ Tell your friend that you will find another way home, encourage him not to drink, and encourage him not to keep the beer in his possession.

What are some of the possible consequences of the decision that you just made?

_____

_____

_____

_____

_____

_____

Name: _____ Date: _____

THE LAW ON ALCOHOL

The decisions that you will make about using or not using alcohol are important, no matter what your age. However, the decisions that you make in your teen and pre-teen years on whether or not to use alcohol and whether or not to be with those who are using alcohol are high-risk because you are under the legal drinking age. The laws relating to the use of alcohol vary from state to state. In many states, laws like the ones listed below apply to teenagers.

- When issuing a traffic citation, a police officer will test for alcohol if the officer believes that the driver has been drinking.
- Those who are caught drinking and driving may lose their driver's licenses, face fines, and serve jail time.
- The loss of a driver's license may vary from a few months to years.

1. What is the law concerning teenagers who are involved with alcohol in your state?

_____

_____

2. In your state, what are the consequences if a police officer catches your under-age friend in possession of alcohol?

_____

_____

3. What are the consequences in your state if your under-age friend is caught with open liquor in the car?

_____

_____

4. In your state, what are the consequences if your under-age friend is caught driving while intoxicated?

_____

_____

5. Even though you are not drinking, what are the consequences in your state if you are caught in a car where there is alcohol?

_____

_____

Name: _____ Date: _____

BLOOD ALCOHOL CONTENT: ITS EFFECT ON YOU

Alcohol effects those who drink. If an individual is driving an automobile, the safety of the driver, passengers, pedestrians, and other motorists may be endangered. The test to determine if the driver of an automobile is legally intoxicated is called the **Blood Alcohol Content**, or BAC. BAC is the amount of alcohol in the bloodstream.

Alcohol is absorbed into the bloodstream mainly through the small intestine. Food in the small intestine or stomach will slow the absorption of alcohol into the bloodstream, but it is important to know that no matter how much alcohol a person drinks, the liver can only metabolize, or burn, one-half ounce of alcohol per hour. The rest of the alcohol remains in the bloodstream until the liver has had time to metabolize the alcohol.

Each state has laws that specify when a drinker is legally intoxicated. Although everyone is affected by the drinking of any amount of alcohol, some individuals become intoxicated before others. Women are generally affected by alcohol more than men are. This is due to the smaller body size of most women, and to the fact that women have a higher percentage of body fat than men. The amount of food consumed prior to drinking also affects intoxication. The more food in the stomach, the longer it takes to become intoxicated. The emotional state of the drinker also affects intoxication.

The National Highway Traffic Safety Administration has published a chart, reprinted on page 92, that can be used as a guide to determine when a person is legally intoxicated.

1. According to the chart, what two factors determine the blood alcohol content?

    _____

2. Underline the statement below that best states the message in the chart.

    A. Consuming any amount of alcohol is a possible safety problem.

    B. There is no problem with drinking unless the BAC is 0.05 or higher.

The liver can metabolize (burn) approximately $\frac{1}{2}$ ounce of liquor per hour. If a person drinks more than that amount, it remains in the bloodstream until the liver can metabolize it. If alcohol is in the bloodstream, it can be measured with the blood alcohol test.

3. How many hours will it take before a drink containing $1\frac{1}{2}$ ounces of alcohol is out of the

    bloodstream? _____

4. If an individual who weighs 200 pounds has three drinks (each containing $1\frac{1}{2}$ ounces of

    alcohol), how many hours will it take before the alcohol is out of the bloodstream? _____

5. How many ounces of 86-proof liquor is one 12-ounce can of beer equal to? _____

6. How many hours will it take for the liver to metabolize the alcohol in two 12-ounce cans of

    beer? _____

Name: _____ Date: _____

AVERAGE EFFECTS OF ALCOHOL

This chart shows average responses to alcohol. Individual responses may differ.

Weight (Pounds)	Drinks in a Two-Hour Period $1\frac{1}{2}$ Ounces 86-Proof Liquor or 12 Ounces Beer											
100	1	2	3	4	5	6	7	8	9	10	11	12
120	1	2	3	4	5	6	7	8	9	10	11	12
140	1	2	3	4	5	6	7	8	9	10	11	12
160	1	2	3	4	5	6	7	8	9	10	11	12
180	1	2	3	4	5	6	7	8	9	10	11	12
200	1	2	3	4	5	6	7	8	9	10	11	12
220	1	2	3	4	5	6	7	8	9	10	11	12
240	1	2	3	4	5	6	7	8	9	10	11	12

Be Careful BAC to 0.05	Driving Impaired BAC 0.05–0.09	Do Not Drive BAC 0.10 and up

Source for information in chart: National Highway Traffic Safety Administration

Name: _____ Date: _____

 # IT'S UP TO YOU: HOW CAN YOU HELP?

Situation:

You have a family member who has begun to show signs that alcohol may be a problem for him or her. Some of the changes that you have noted are frequent mood changes, a drop in school attendance and grades, problems at school and home over alcohol, tardiness or absence from work, and a desire to associate with those who drink or use drugs.

The statements below are some of the actions that you might take. Place a plus (+) by the ways that you can best help this individual.

_____ Make excuses that the individual has problems because of the pressures of his or her job.

_____ Accuse the individual of being a drunk.

_____ Blame the crowd the individual spends the most time with.

_____ Be a good listener to find out the reasons why there might be a problem.

_____ Tell the individual that he/she is a very weak person.

_____ Try to assist the individual in getting help.

Look at a diagram of the human body that shows the organs (ask your teacher for one, or look for one in your health or science book or an encyclopedia). List the organs that are affected by the use of illegal drugs, alcohol, and tobacco and by the overuse or misuse of legal drugs.

_____

_____

_____

_____

_____

_____

_____

Now is the time for you to develop safe, healthy, and responsible habits that you can have for the rest of your life. Just say no!

Name: _____ Date: _____

DECISION MAKING: WORTH THE RISK?

The decisions you make in life always involve some risk. Some decisions that you make may involve great risk for your health, your self-esteem, your chance to be successful in life, and your happiness. However, it is always possible to make decisions that are less likely to be harmful to you and your future.

Many times decisions that involve great risk are made because people do not understand the risk that is being taken. Often when poor decisions are made, it is because people do not have all of the information that they need, and they fail to get that information before they decide. People sometimes engage in risky behavior because they are not willing to stand up for the things that they know are right. Some feel that it is easier to let others make decisions for them. Sometimes decisions are made involving risk when people do not believe that they can control their own destinies.

If you are going to make good decisions, you must know what things are important to you. You need to think about your willingness to stand up for the things that you believe are right. You must think about the things that you value. When you choose to make a decision to do something that you believe or know is wrong, you need to understand why you are willing to go along with such a decision. You are the one who must think about your decisions. You are the one who must determine if the decisions you make will be in your best interest or if they will only please someone else.

The following list of questions is designed to help you begin to think about your decision-making process. You may or may not want to discuss your answers with other people. However, to make good decisions, you must begin to identify how and why you make a decision. The things that you value determine the kinds of decisions that you will make. Read each of the following statements. If the item is important to you, place a plus (+) on the blank. If the item is not important to you, place a minus (-) on the blank.

_____ 1. I would like to have more friends.
_____ 2. I would like to have more confidence.
_____ 3. I would like to have better clothes.
_____ 4. I would like to lose weight.
_____ 5. I would like to have more energy.
_____ 6. I would like to make better grades.
_____ 7. I like lots of pizza, sandwiches, candy, soda, and fast foods.
_____ 8. I enjoy exercise.
_____ 9. I spend lots of time watching television and resting.
_____ 10. I would like to improve my physical appearance.
_____ 11. Pleasing my friends is important to me.
_____ 12. Pleasing my parent(s) is important to me.
_____ 13. Preparing for my future is important to me.
_____ 14. Pleasing my teachers is important to me.
_____ 15. Being a good worker is important to me.

Name: _____ Date: _____

GETTING TO KNOW YOU

The following diagram is designed to help you learn something about yourself. In the large middle circle, write your name. In the small ovals surrounding it, write words that you would like your friends to use to describe you.

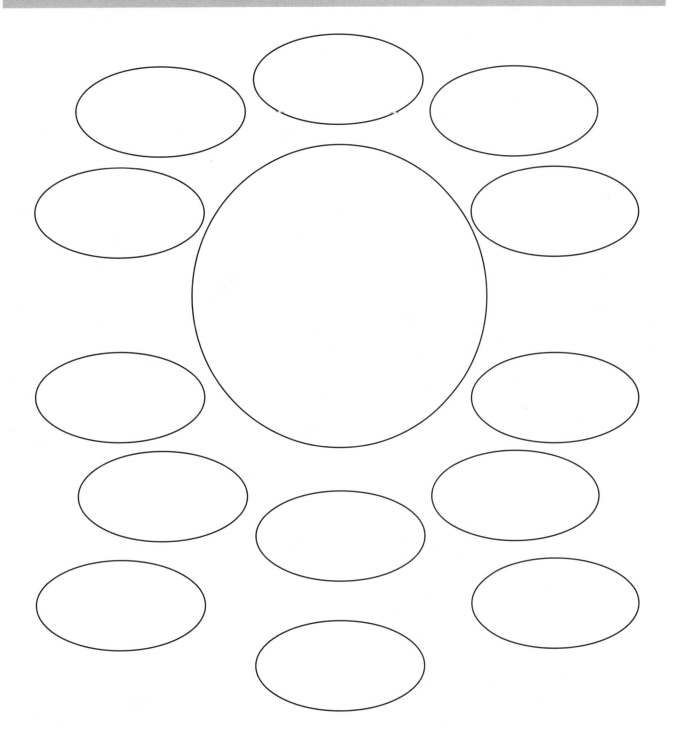

Name: _____ Date: _____

GETTING TO KNOW YOU (cont.)

This graph is similar to the one on the previous page. Put your name in the large central circle. Then write words that you would like your parent(s) and teachers to use to describe you in the smaller surrounding ovals.

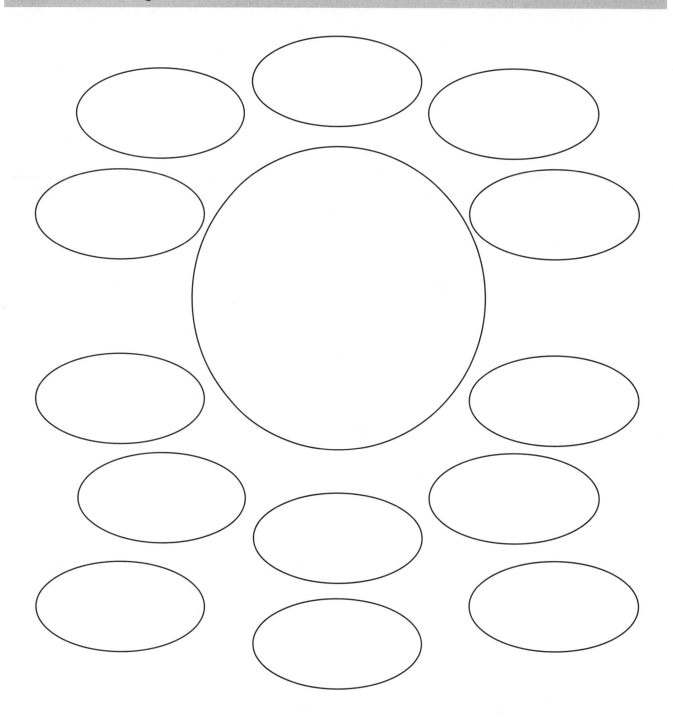

Name: _____ Date: _____

STEREOTYPES: WHAT DO YOU THINK?

For the following activity, place a plus (+) in front of the statements with which you agree. Place a minus (-) in front of the statements with which you disagree.

_____ 1. I believe that there are jobs that only women should do and jobs that only men should do.

_____ 2. I think that people who do not look me in the eye have something to hide.

_____ 3. I think that everyone should sit quietly and listen to what the teacher has to say.

_____ 4. I think that most immigrants prefer to live in their own communities.

_____ 5. I think that most people who have the same colored skin should stay together.

_____ 6. I think that some races are smarter than others.

_____ 7. I think that most immigrants would rather cling to their old ways than become Americans.

_____ 8. I think that if people don't want to work hard and try to get ahead, they shouldn't be allowed to become American citizens.

_____ 9. I think that people should all wear the same kinds of clothes.

_____ 10. I think that the American way of life is best for everyone.

_____ 11. I think that Americans can learn a lot from other cultures.

_____ 12. I think it is all right for people not to speak English in their homes, but that in public everyone should speak English.

_____ 13. I think that people who work hard are better people than those who don't work hard.

_____ 14. I think that people who do not try to get ahead are lazy.

_____ 15. I think that the more educated you are, the better person you are.

_____ 16. I think that people in other countries all want to come to the United States.

_____ 17. It irritates me when people don't speak my language.

_____ 18. Individuals who mind and respect their parents irritate me.

_____ 19. People who wear bright colors irritate me.

_____ 20. I don't want to try foods from other cultures.

_____ 21. I want to know what part of town someone lives in before I want him or her for a friend.

_____ 22. I think that my friends should be more loyal to me than to their parents.

_____ 23. Some cultural groups speak loudly and that irritates me.

_____ 24. Some cultural groups physically move around a lot and that irritates me.

_____ 25. I think that since some foreign groups work hard and try to get ahead, they are better suited for citizenship than other foreign groups.

_____ 26. I like to have a doctor whose skin is the same color as mine.

_____ 27. I like to have a teacher whose skin is the same color as mine.

Most of the statements above are about what you think, like, or feel. Often such thoughts and feelings are based on inaccurate information about others. A large number of pluses in the list above might indicate that you are prejudiced and misinformed about others. Many times, the misconceptions and biases are a result of stereotyping a group by the actions of an individual.

Name: _____ Date: _____

AMERICAN MELTING POT

Match the statement on the left with the word that best represents that statement on the right.

_____ 1. understanding and appreciation of others
_____ 2. refers to the view that one race is superior to another
_____ 3. when two groups of people with different lifestyles
do not appreciate each other
_____ 4. the way a group of people work, live, and
pass on their way of life
_____ 5. unfavorable opinion of another group often formed
without adequate information
_____ 6. one who believes that his or her sex is more capable
than the other
_____ 7. the difference among cultural groups
_____ 8. designating groups of people based on their customs,
language, food, clothing, etc.

A. status
B. prejudice
C. chauvinist
D. ethnic
E. culture
F. ethnocentrism
G. empathy
H. cultural diversity
I. cultural conflict

In the following activity place a plus (+) by those things with which you agree.
Place a minus (-) by the ones with which you disagree.

_____ 9. The hamburger is an American food.
_____ 10. Corn was developed and first grown by Americans.
_____ 11. Basketball is a sport that was invented in America.
_____ 12. The delicatessen was first founded in America.
_____ 13. The word *tycoon,* meaning an important businessman
of great wealth, originated in America.
_____ 14. Kindergarten is an American idea.
_____ 15. When people dance a waltz, they are dancing an American dance.
_____ 16. The idea of a patio is an American idea.
_____ 17. When you eat an enchilada, you are eating an American food.
_____ 18. Spaghetti was first eaten in America.
_____ 19. The *ghetto* is an American word that came into being when
immigrants arrived here.
_____ 20. When you wear moccasins, you are wearing something that was first worn in
America.
_____ 21. When the early settlers first came to America, they named the small striped animal
chipmunk.
_____ 22. The word *yacht,* used to describe a pleasure boat, is a term that originated in
America.
_____ 23. Sauerkraut was first eaten in America.
_____ 24. Cole slaw was first eaten in America.
_____ 25. Independence Day is celebrated on July 4 only in America.

The United States is a unique country. A large part of the language and culture of the
United States is a result of the immigrants who contributed words, customs, and ideas to the
rest of the nation. No wonder it has been called the "melting pot"!

Name: _____ Date: _____

SMALL WORLD

In each community in the United States, there are examples of the contributions of other cultures. Buildings, foods, clothing, language, values, and religious beliefs are reminders of the cultural heritage of individual communities.

Think about things in your community that are examples of the influence of other cultures. List them below. Don't forget things that your own family does or says!

_____

_____

_____

_____

Many times opinions are formed about groups of people based on inadequate information or because of unfamiliarity. Often we fail to realize that humankind is more alike than different. We recognize that individuals within our own group differ, but often assume that the individuals in another group are very much alike.

Study each of the groups that are listed below. Try to find out where they lived, how they lived, when they lived, and any unique accomplishments that they have made. Then answer the questions that follow.

United States today
West African civilizations in Ghana, Mali, and Songhai
Incan civilization
Middle Eastern civilizations
Roman civilization

1. List some of the great accomplishments of each of these civilizations.

_____

_____

_____

_____

_____

_____

Name: _____ Date: _____

SMALL WORLD (cont.)

2. List some of the things that arc similar about these civilizations.

_____

_____

_____

_____

_____

3. List some of the things that are unique about each of these civilizations.

_____

_____

_____

_____

_____

Complete the following statements with the information that you learned from your research.

4. These civilizations all _____.

5. These civilizations were _____.

6. The citizens in each civilization _____.

7. The leaders of these civilizations _____.

8. The physical features of the people _____.

    People are more alike than different. Physical characteristics and observed social behaviors often cause us to stereotype groups unfairly. The United States is not simply a land of people with specific physical or social characteristics. It is a land of people from all over the world who have contributed parts of their culture, language, ideas, and achievements to make it a greater nation.

Name: _____   Date: _____

YOUR FUTURE: DARE TO DREAM

Complete the following sentences with the statement that first comes to mind.

I admire people who _____.

I like to _____.

If I could, I would _____.

Happy people _____.

Someday I _____.

I wish _____.

When I graduate, I want _____.

I feel good when I _____.

When I work, I _____.

In developing better decision-making skills, it is often important to think about your future and the kind of job you would like to have. Look at the following list of jobs and place a plus (+) in front of each job that you might enjoy. Place a star (*) in front of the job that you most want to try.

_____ teacher	_____ secretary	_____ computer analyst
_____ hotel clerk	_____ travel guide	_____ construction worker
_____ landscape architect	_____ athletic coach	_____ choreographer
_____ medical technician	_____ biochemist	_____ conservationist
_____ real estate agent	_____ carpenter	_____ dental assistant
_____ plumber	_____ auto body repairman	_____ executive housekeeper
_____ nurse practitioner	_____ child care worker	_____ farm machinery mechanic
_____ truck driver	_____ cashier	_____ fashion designer
_____ architect	_____ chemist	_____ flight attendant
_____ pilot	_____ politician	_____ doctor
_____ lawyer	_____ author	_____ web designer

Talk to your teacher, counselor, parents, or someone in the job you have chosen to find out what school subjects are helpful in preparing for this job. Write the classes that you will need to take in the blanks below.

_____

_____

_____

_____

Name: _____ Date: _____

YOUR FUTURE: DARE TO DREAM (cont.)

In addition to the courses you must take in school, what are some other skills that you will need for the job?

_____	work well with other people	_____	meet new people
_____	travel	_____	work long hours
_____	listen to other points of view	_____	be my own boss
_____	help make decisions	_____	give my opinions
_____	work with people unlike me	_____	solve problems
_____	work weekends	_____	work inside
_____	take orders from others	_____	make my own schedule
_____	continue education	_____	work by myself
_____	work outside	_____	work in dust and dirt
_____	work in a very clean environment	_____	lift heavy objects
_____	meet deadlines	_____	repeat the same task over and over
_____	look for creative solutions	_____	be away from family
_____	dress in suit and tie or other nice clothes		

  Now that you have chosen an occupation and looked at some of the skills and working conditions of that job, you are closer to making a decision about it. Go to your library or guidance office or use the Internet to find out what the average starting salary is, how many jobs are predicted to be available in that area when you graduate, where the jobs are most likely to be located, and any other interesting information about the career you have selected.

  Making a decision about the kind of work you would enjoy when you are out of school is important. In thinking about the kind of work that you might enjoy, you need to consider some other things. For example, what are some of the things that you want the job to provide for you beyond the money for food and clothing? Think of some things that you would like to own, enjoy, and have the finances to do when you have completed school and are working full time. List these in the blanks below.

_____

_____

_____

_____

_____

_____

Name: _____ Date: _____

EMPLOYEE DECISIONS

The United States has been called the land of opportunity—a land where anyone can have a better life if he or she will work. The United States is still a land of opportunity, but today, workers must be willing to do more than just work hard. Place a plus (+) by those things that you think are important if you are to be a successful employee.

_____ work cooperatively with others

_____ have good reading, writing, and math skills

_____ identify problems and suggest solutions

_____ be late or absent from work most of the time

_____ wait for the supervisor's direction before doing any task

_____ do not try to get along with other employees, just do your own work well

_____ know the right people but don't work hard

_____ know the right people instead of having the necessary job skills

_____ be dependable

_____ be punctual

_____ be a self-starter

_____ be careful not to do more than is expected

_____ look for ways to improve the company

_____ be willing to ignore other workers' actions, such as using drugs and alcohol on the job

_____ be willing to improve personal job skills

Name: _____ Date: _____

YOU CHOOSE: PLANNING FOR THE FUTURE

Situation 1:

You have decided that you would like to be a _____. If you can get the training and secure a job that you think you will like, the work and the salary will allow you to have some of the things that you want. You are a hard worker and are willing to take the courses to prepare for the job. However, when you are about to enroll for the courses, you meet a trusted friend who tells you to take the same courses that he or she is taking. Then you will have more free time and will not have to do so much work. You know that the courses your friend is suggesting will not prepare you for the career that you want. However, this is a close friend and he or she will be upset if you do not take the courses that he or she is suggesting.

Read the following statements and place a plus (+) beside the decision that is most like the one that you would make.

_____ Tell your friend that you need the courses for your career and that you must enroll as planned.

_____ Tell your friend why you are taking the courses and invite him or her to enroll in the courses with you.

_____ Accept your friend's suggestion and enroll in the courses with him or her.

_____ Tell your friend that the courses he or she is suggesting may allow more free time now but that you will be unprepared for a career and you do not intend for that to happen.

_____ Tell your friend that you really want to take the courses you had planned on but that his or her friendship is so important that you will enroll in the courses with him/her.

_____ Explain to your friend that you must enroll in the courses as you planned, but you are sure that there will be plenty of time for you to spend together.

Name: _____ Date: _____

YOU CHOOSE: PLANNING FOR THE FUTURE (cont.)

Situation 2:

You have enrolled in the courses to prepare for the career that you want. You have to work hard, but the courses are going well. You feel that if you attend class and do the homework, you can maintain a passing grade. Your friend meets you in the hallway and tells you that there will be a party that evening. He or she insists that you come to the party and says that if you don't, no one will waste time by inviting you in the future. You have an important test the next day and know that you should study.

Read the following statements and place a plus (+) in front of the statement that is most like what you would do.

_____ Tell your friend that you are sorry but that you must stay home and prepare for the exam.

_____ Tell your friend that you will be at the party.

_____ Tell your friend that you need to study but that you would like to attend in the future when you can.

_____ Tell your friend that the exam is more important than the party and that you intend to do well on the exam.

_____ Thank your friend and walk away.

Situation 3:

You are on your way to class and you meet your best friend and some other close friends who are also in the hallway. One of them speaks to you, but you hear your best friend say: "Forget him. He thinks he's going to be a big shot someday. We don't need jerks like him at our parties."

Read each of the following statements and place a plus (+) in front of the statement that is most like what you would do.

_____ Ignore the group and continue on to class.

_____ Speak to the friend who spoke and continue to class.

_____ Stop and speak to each member of the group and ask them how things are going.

_____ Stop and speak to each member of the group and tell your best friend that you don't intend to be a big shot, but you do need to take certain classes to have the career that you want, and you intend to attend your classes and do well in them.

_____ Stop and speak to each member of the group and tell your best friend that you are sorry that he feels the way he does.

Name: _____ Date: _____

PAYING FOR A LOAN

Understanding finances can be an important part of a healthy lifestyle. Today, most of us borrow money and make monthly payments. When we get a loan, we must pay interest. The amount of the loan is called the **principal**. **Interest** is the fee that is paid to borrow the principal. It is important to pay off the outstanding loan principal and the interest. If a principal payment and interest is paid each month, then the amount of principal decreases each month. If you only make payments on the interest, then the principal amount that you borrowed is never paid back.

Example:

A loan is made in the amount of $1,200. The $1,200 is the principal. The interest to be paid for the $1,200 is 5%. The loan period is 12 months, or 1 year. The loan is to be repaid in 12 equal monthly payments of $100 plus the 5% interest on the principal each month.

Monthly Repayment Schedule

Month	1st	2nd	3rd	4th	5th	6th	7th	8th	9th	10th	11th	12th
Principal	$1,200	$1,100	$1,000	$900	$800	$700	$600	$500	$400	$300	$200	$100
Interest Paid	$5	$4.58	$4.16	$3.75	$3.33	$2.91	$2.50	$2.27	$1.81	$1.25	$0.83	$0.41

Total Monthly Payment Due

1st	2nd	3rd	4th	5th	6th	7th	8th	9th	10th	11th	12th
$105	$104.58	$104.16	$103.75	$103.33	$102.91	$102.50	$102.27	$101.81	$101.25	$100.83	$100.41

Add the total interest paid for the 12-month loan.

$5 + $4.58 + $4.16 + $3.75 + $3.33 + $2.91 + $2.50 + $2.27 + $1.81 + $1.25 + $0.83 + $0.41 = $_____

Why would the interest paid not be $60 for the $1,200 loan? [$1,200 • 0.05 = $60] You did not have $1,200 borrowed for the entire 12 months. Each month, your principal decreased by $100. At the end of each month, that was the principal you owed the 5% interest on. You had an <u>approximate</u> amount of $600 borrowed for the 12 month period.

A quick way to determine the interest you should pay on a loan is to determine the interest rate and then determine the <u>average</u> amount of the loan for the loan period. In the case of a $1,200 loan for 12 months, the average loan amount for the 12-month period is approximately $600. [$600 • 0.05 = $30] This is the approximate interest amount you should pay for the loan for the year.

Name: _____ Date: _____

PAYING FOR A LOAN (cont.)

1. Find the average amount borrowed and the approximate interest amount for each of the following.

    a) $600 for 12 months at 5% interest.

    The average amount borrowed for 12 months _____

    Approximate interest to be paid _____

    b) $1,800 for 12 months at 6% interest.

    The average amount borrowed for 12 months _____

    Approximate interest to be paid _____

    c) $2,400 for 12 months at 8% interest.

    The average amount borrowed for 12 months _____

    Approximate interest to be paid _____

2. Many times, the amount borrowed is for more than 12 months. Then the principal amount and interest must be figured for the longer period. The approximate principal amount and approximate interest charge can be found.

    Example: $1,200 is borrowed for 24 months at an interest rate of 4%.

    The approximate amount borrowed for the 24 months is $600. The interest is $600 • 0.04 = $24. However, the loan is for 24 months, or 2 years. So the $24 interest amount must be multiplied by 2. $24 • 2 = $48 This is the approximate amount of interest that should be paid for the $600 loan for the 2-year period.

    Find the following.

    a) $1,800 for 18 months at 5% interest

    The average amount borrowed for 1.5 years _____

    Approximate interest to be paid _____

    b) $1,800 for 24 months at 6% interest

    The average amount borrowed for 2 years _____

    Approximate interest to be paid _____

    c) $2,400 for 36 months at 7% interest

    The average amount borrowed for 3 years _____

    Approximate interest to be paid _____

    d) $3,000 for 48 months at 6% interest

    The average amount borrowed for 4 years _____

    Approximate interest to be paid _____

Name: _____ Date: _____

BUYING AN AUTO

Car Depreciation

A common option is to buy a car with a 60-month loan. As you have learned, the longer it takes to pay back a loan, the more money you pay in interest. It is important to remember that a car depreciates, or decreases, in value after it is purchased. When the pay period is over an extended time, the depreciated value of the car may be less than the amount still owed on the car. This is called being upside-down on a loan. One way being upside-down can cause problems is if you are in an accident. The insurance that covers the car if wrecked is based on the depreciated value of the car. The insurance company will pay the depreciated value of the car. If you owe more money than the amount paid by the insurance, you are still responsible to make the payments on a car that you don't drive anymore. Therefore, it makes sense to use a shorter time period to pay for the car. The monthly payments will be larger, but it is more likely that the depreciated value of the car and the amount owed will be closer to the same amount.

Let's say you buy a car for $24,000. The car will depreciate each year, which means it will be worth less money. A question you must ask is: How much must I pay each month so that the insurance will cover the amount owed if the car is wrecked?

Example: A car is purchased for $24,000. The car is financed for 60 months at 4.9% interest. The monthly payment is $400 plus interest, which is an additional $9.80 a month. The car is wrecked after 24 months with $9,835.20 paid. The depreciated value of the car is $13,000. The insurance company issues a check for $13,000. The $9,835.20 + $13,000 equals $22,835.20. The $22,835.20 does not equal the $24,000 plus the total interest of $588. The owner of the car is responsible for paying the difference between $24,588 and $22,835.20, which is $1,752.80.

Solve the following.

1. You purchase a car for $24,000. The car is financed for 60 months at 5%. The monthly payment is $400 plus interest, which is an additional $_____. The car is wrecked after 24 months with $9,840 paid. The insurance company will pay $12,000, the depreciated value of the car. The amount that has been paid on the car is $_____. The amount owed on the loan after the wreck is $_____. The difference between what the insurance company paid and the amount owed on the car is $_____. After the insurance company payment, you still owe $_____.

2. Your friend purchases a car for $24,000. The car is financed for 48 months at 5%. The monthly payment is $500 plus interest, which is an additional $_____. The car is wrecked after 24 months with $12,300 paid. The insurance company will pay $12,000, the depreciated value of the car. The amount that has been paid on the car is $_____. The amount owed on the loan after the wreck is $_____. The difference between what the insurance company paid and the amount owed on the car is $_____. After the insurance company payment, your friend still owes $_____.

Name: _____ Date: _____

BUYING AN AUTO (cont.)

You find a car that you really want, and you can afford to pay the price. You have worked out the financing so you can pay an amount each month that protects you from owing a debt if the car is wrecked. There are other expenses that you will have to pay in addition to the cost of the car. There may be a state tax and even a local tax. The license for the car and insurance are also extra. When you are making a car purchase, you must check with the automobile company to find what the additional expenses will be.

Computing Car Costs

Cost of car: $10,000	$10,000
State tax on car cost: 7% of the amount financed, or 0.07 • $10,000	$700
License: $75	$75
Insurance: $500	$500
Total you must have available to buy the car:	$11,275

You plan to buy a car that costs $20,000 where you live. Research to find out what your state and local taxes, license fees, and cost of insurance would be. Complete the blanks below to find the costs you would have to consider when purchasing a car.

My State: _____   City: _____

Cost of car: $20,000

Insurance: $_____

License: $_____

State tax: $_____   Tax percentage 0.0____ • $20,000 = State Tax

Local tax: $_____   Tax percentage 0.0____ • $20,000 = Local Tax

Other: $_____

Total: $_____

Name: _____ Date: _____

FIGURING THE COST FOR GAS

After buying a car, you will have the expense of maintaining it. Gas to operate the car will be a big expense. When figuring your weekly expenses, you must include the cost of gas as a major item.

Circle the correct answers for the following.

John drives his car 25 miles, seven days each week. His car gets 14 miles per each gallon of gas. John buys his gas for $3.50 per gallon.

1. John will drive his car a total of

    a) 100   **b)** 150   **c)** 175   **d)** 200   miles each week.

2. John must buy   **a)** 12.5   **b)** 14   **c)** 15.5   **d)** 18.5   gallons of gas each week.

3. John will spend   **a)** $40.50   **b)** $43.75   **c)** $45.50   **d)** $46.00   for gas each week.

Tiauana drives her car 42 miles, seven days each week. Her car gets 14 miles per each gallon of gas. Tiauana buys her gas for $3.75 per gallon.

4. Tiauana will drive her car a total of   **a)** 275   **b)** 294   **c)** 300   **d)** 314   miles each week.

5. Tiauana must buy   **a)** 12   **b)** 16   **c)** 19   **d)** 21   gallons of gas each week.

6. Tiauana will spend   **a)** $60.50   **b)** $78.75   **c)** $85.50   **d)** $88.25   for gas each

    week.

Mary drives her car 35 miles, six days a week. Her car gets 30 miles per each gallon of gas. Mary buys her gas for $2.95 per gallon.

7. Mary will drive her car a total of   **a)** 210   **b)** 240   **c)** 250   **d)** 300   miles each week.

8. Mary must buy   **a)** 5.5   **b)** 6   **c)** 7   **d)** 9.5   gallons of gas each week.

9. Mary will spend   **a)** $15.75   **b)** $16.32   **c)** $18.89   **d)** $20.65   for gas each week.

Name: _____ Date: _____

SOCIAL SECURITY TRUST FUND

Someday, you will retire. As you get older, living a healthy lifestyle will be more important than ever if you are to maintain good health. Managing your health and finances now are key to enjoying a long and happy retirement. You must make sure you have enough money saved to pay for healthy foods, a comfortable place to live, and adequate medical care. If you take care of your health and money properly, you can enjoy the golden years. To maintain a healthy lifestyle into your retirement years, you must begin to develop a financial plan while you are young.

In the United States, most workers must pay Social Security tax. The tax is taken out of your paycheck and sent to the federal government. The money is then placed in the Social Security Trust Fund, from which you will be paid when you retire. At this time, the Social Security tax is 12.4% of your salary. An additional Medicare tax of 2.90% must be paid from your salary. The total tax for Social Security and Medicare is 12.4% + 2.90% = 15.3% of your salary.

If you work for someone else, you pay a tax rate of 6.2% from your salary for Social Security and 1.45% for Medicare tax. Your employer also pays 6.2% for your Social Security tax and 1.45% Medicare tax for you.

If you are self-employed, you must pay the total 12.4% Social Security tax and 2.90% Medicare tax.

Complete the following activities.

1. You are employed by ABC Company. Complete the following to find how much money must come out of your weekly paycheck.

		Weekly Salary	x	Tax Rate	
a.	Social Security Tax	$400	x	0.062	= _____
b.	Medicare Tax	$400	x	0.0145	= _____
c.	Total Tax Paid Weekly				= _____

Your take-home pay for the week would be $369.40. The ABC Company would also pay $30.60 for your Social Security and Medicare taxes.

If you are self-employed and earned $400 each week, you would pay 12.4% for Social Security tax and 2.90% for Medicare tax, for a total each week of $61.20.

Name: _____ Date: _____

SOCIAL SECURITY TRUST FUND (cont.)

2. You work for XYZ company. Your weekly check is $500. Complete the blanks for payments for the Social Security tax and Medicare tax.

Weekly Salary	Social Security Tax	+	Medicare Tax	=	Amount Paid
a. $500 (You pay)	$_____	+	$_____	=	$_____
b. $500 (XYZ pays)	$_____	+	$_____	=	$_____
c. Total for "a" and "b"	$_____	+	$_____	=	$_____

3. You are a carpenter working for yourself, which means you are self-employed. You earn $500 each week. Compete the following to show the amount of Social Security and Medicare tax you must pay.

	Weekly Salary	x	Tax Rate	
a. Social Security Tax	$500	x	0.124	= _____
b. Medicare Tax	$500	x	0.029	= _____
c. Total Tax Paid Weekly				= _____

d. What is your take-home pay for the week? _____

Name: _____ Date: _____

SOCIAL SECURITY TRUST FUND (cont.)

Retirement Age

The following chart shows the age at which a worker can retire and receive full Social Security benefits. Fill in the blanks to complete the statements that follow.

Year of Birth	Age for Full Retirement Benefits
1937	65 years
1938	65 years 2 months
1939	65 years 4 months
1940	65 years 6 months
1941	65 years 8 months
1942	65 years 10 months
1943–54	66 years
1955	66 years 2 months
1956	66 years 4 months
1957	66 years 6 months
1958	66 years 8 months
1959	66 years 10 months
1960–later	67 years

1. My birth date is _____. I will be 67 years of age in the year _____.

2. Someone born January 1, 1958, would be eligible for full retirement benefits in the year

   _____.

3. Someone born October 20, 1978, would be eligible for full retirement benefits in the year

   _____.

4. Someone born December 4, 1955, would be eligible for full retirement benefits in the year

   _____.

Earning Social Security Credits

To be eligible to draw Social Security when you reach retirement age, you must earn 40 credits. You earn 1 credit for every $920 you earn. The limit of earned credits is 4 per year. If you earn 4 credits per each year worked, then after working for 10 years, you would be eligible to receive full Social Security benefits when you are old enough to retire.

Name: _____ Date: _____

INVESTMENTS TO BUILD MY RETIREMENT FUND

Unfortunately, Social Security will not provide enough money for most people to live on at retirement. Therefore, it is wise to have a saving plan that will give you extra retirement money. The following are only three of the possible ways to save for retirement.

Savings Accounts

Many people have a savings account at their bank. Each month, the bank pays interest on the amount of money in the savings account. You will want to know if your bank is paying simple interest or compound interest on your savings account.

Simple Interest

The money you place in a savings account is the **principal**. The bank pays an interest rate on the principal. **Interest** is the amount of money the bank pays you for depositing money in their bank and letting them use it. The formula for figuring how much interest you are earning is:

interest rate x principal = amount earned on savings account.

Example: José places $2,000 in his savings account. The bank pays a simple interest rate of 3% on his $2,000 savings. Change the 3% to the decimal 0.03 and use the formula for finding simple interest.

0.03 x $2,000 = $60

At the end of one year, José will have $2,060 in his savings account.

Find the following for savings accounts at simple interest.

1. Judy places $2,000 in savings at 4% interest for one year.

   0._____ x $_____ = $_____

2. At the end of the year, Judy will have $_____ in her savings account.

3. Michai places $3,000 in savings at 3% interest for one year.

   0._____ x $_____ = $_____

4. At the end of the year, Michai will have $_____ in his savings account.

5. Waldo places $2,500 in savings at 4% interest for one year.

   0._____ x $_____ = $_____

6. At the end of the year, Waldo will have $_____ in his savings account.

Name: _____ Date: _____

INVESTMENTS TO BUILD MY RETIREMENT FUND (cont.)

Compound Interest

You can make more money on your savings account if the interest on your principal is **compounded**. This means the bank calculates the interest more than once a year, adds the interest to the principal, and then uses that total to calculate the interest the next time.

Example: You place $2,000 in a savings account with the interest compounded quarterly, or every three months. If the interest rate is 4%, then every quarter, or three months, you will have 1% interest added to your principal. The 4% is divided by 4 because the interest will be figured four times throughout the year. This gives us the 1% interest rate.

The $2,000 principal at the end of the first three months would earn an interest payment of $20.00 (0.01 x $2,000 = $20). The $20 interest is added to your principal, so for the next three months, you would be paid interest on a principal of $2,020.

The $2,020 principal at the end of the second three months would earn an interest payment of $20.20 (0.01 x $2,020 = $20.20). The $20.20 interest is added to your principal of $2,020, so for the next three months, you would be paid interest on a principal of $2,040.20.

The $2,040.20 principal at the end of the third quarter, or three-month period, would earn an interest payment of $20.40 (0.01 x $2,040.20 = $20.40). The $20.40 interest is added to your principal of $2,040.20, so for the next three months, you would be paid interest on a principal of $2,060.60.

The $2,060.60 principal at the end of the third quarter would earn an interest payment of $20.60 (0.01 x $2,060.60 = $20.60). The $20.60 is added to your principal of $2,060.60, making the total principal for the year $2081.21 ($2,060.60 + $20.60 = $2,081.20). The $2,000 principal earned interest of $81.20 for the year.

If the $2,000 had been placed in a savings account paying 4% simple interest, the interest earned for the year would have been $80.00

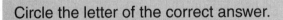

Circle the letter of the correct answer.

1. If simple interest and compound interest pay the same interest rate, it is best to invest savings in a   **a)** simple interest   **b)** compound interest   savings account.

2. If the simple interest rate for the year is 6%, what would the interest rate be if the interest were compounded monthly? (Hint: Divide the 6% by the number of months in a year.)

   a) 1%   **b)** 12%   **c)** 0.6%   **d)** 0.5%

Name: _____ Date: _____

INVESTMENTS TO BUILD MY RETIREMENT FUND (cont.)

Certificates of Deposit

Certificates of Deposit (also called CDs) are a safe way to save. They are usually sold in amounts of $1,000 and up. CDs pay a stated rate of interest for the investment period chosen. CDs usually pay a higher rate of interest than a savings account because you are agreeing to keep your money in the bank for a certain period of time. There is a penalty if you decide to cash in your CD before the time period is up. Usually the time periods are from six months to five years. After the time period is up, you can buy another CD for a new time period. The interest rate may be different for the new time period. CDs are safe because they are guaranteed by the U.S. government.

Example: Franco places $1,000 in a CD for one year. The interest rate is 5%. At the end of the year, the CD will mature, and Franco will receive $1,050.

0.05 x $1,000 = $50 $1,000 + $50 = $1,050

Solve the following.

1. Mike places $1,000 in a CD for one year. The interest rate is 4%.

   0._____ x $1,000 = $_____ + $1,000 = $_____

   At the end of the year, the CD will mature, and Mike will receive $_____.

2. Malisha places $2,000 in a CD for one year. The interest rate is 6%.

   0._____ x $2,000 = $_____ + $2,000 = $_____

   At the end of the year, the CD will mature, and Malisha will receive $_____.

3. Juan places $3,000 in a CD for one year. The interest rate is 5%.

   0._____ x $3,000 = $_____ + $3,000 = $_____

   At the end of the year, the CD will mature, and Juan will receive $_____.

Mutual Funds

Mutual funds are made up of a large number of different stocks. Mutual funds are a good way to invest for most people. These funds are purchased from a fund manager who watches the fund and advises the investors. The value of the mutual fund may change as the stock market goes up or down. However, over long periods of time, a mutual fund is a good investment for retirement.

Name: _____ Date: _____

PLANNING FOR RETIREMENT: ASSESSMENT

Circle or fill in the correct answer that completes each of the following statements.

1. A person born in 1955 must be   a) 66 years

   b) 66 years, 2 months   c) 66 years, 10 months

   d) 67 years   of age to retire with full Social Security benefits.

2. A person born in 1970 must be   a) 65   b) 67   c) 69   d) 71

   years of age to retire with full Social Security benefits.

3. A person born in 1980 will be eligible to retire with full Social Security benefits in

   a) 2017.   b) 2027.   c) 2037.   d) 2047.

4. One Social Security credit is earned for each   a) $620.   b) $920.   c) $1,120.

   d) $1,420.

5. The maximum number of credits you can earn each year is   a) 1.   b) 2.   c) 3.   d) 4.

6. A principal of $2,000 is placed in a savings account that draws a simple interest rate of

   4%. The principal and interest at the end of one year will be

   a) $2,040.   b) $2,060.   c) $2,080.   d) $3,000.

7. A principal of $2,000 is placed in a savings account that draws an interest rate of 4% and

   is compounded quarterly. The principal and interest at the end of one year will be

   a) $2,060.10.   b) $2,080.40.   c) $2,081.20.   d) $2,100.50.

8. A Certificate of Deposit is purchased in the amount of $2,000 for a one-year period. The

   interest paid is 4%. When the CD matures at the end of one year, the principal and interest

   received will be a total of $_____.

9. Mutual funds are an investment in   a) Certificates of Deposit.   b) a bank savings account.

   c) the stock market.

10. The value of a mutual fund   a) goes up and down   b) stays the same

    c) continues to go up   over time.

ANSWER KEYS

Antioxidants (pg. 1)

1–2. Answers will vary.
3. A. Flavonoid: blueberries, purple grapes, apples, cranberries, strawberries, tea, dark chocolate, grape juice, red berries, soybeans, raspberries
B. Lycopene: red tomatoes
C. Lutein: brussels sprouts, spinach, broccoli
D. Carotenoid: carrots
E. Lignan: flax seeds

Finding the Number of Calories From Fat (pg. 3)

1. 560		2. 560; 39.2	
3. 700		4. 700; 49	
5. 875		6. 875; 61.25	

Fat Cloze Exercise (pg. 4)

1. fat	2. saturated
3. cholesterol	4. limited
5. polyunsaturated	6. plant
7. omega-3	
8./9. salmon/herring	10. walnuts
11. fat	12. hydrogen
13. cholesterol	14. hydrogenated
15. shortening	16. limited

Sources of Fat: Graphic Organizer (pg. 5)

Saturated: hot dogs, cheese, whole milk, palm oil, butter
Monounsaturated: olive oil, canola oil
Polyunsaturated: corn, sunflower seeds, soybean oil
Trans Fat: cookies, crackers, chips, cakes, bread

Reviewing Fat: Graphic Organizer (pg. 6)

1. fats
2. saturated fats
3. animal fat/some vegetable oils
4. solid at room temperature

5. problems with too much
6., 7., or 8.   heart disease, stroke, fatty buildup in arteries
9. unsaturated fats
10. most vegetable oils
11. liquid at room temperature

Weighty Matters (pg. 7–8)

1. Fat: hamburger, hot dog, butter, pizza, french fries, potato chips
Protein: hamburger, hot dog, fried chicken, taco, pizza, potato chips
Carbohydrates: hamburger, spaghetti, banana, apple, grapefruit, taco, pizza, french fries, ice cream bar
2–5. Answers will vary.
Teacher check artery diagrams.

Protein, Carbohydrates, and Fiber

Protein (pg. 10)

1. nonessential	2. proteins
3. beans	4. lean
5. ounces	6. cholesterol
7. meat	
8. cell	9. muscle
10. growth	11. protein
12. fat	13. overweight
14. height	

Carbohydrates (pg. 11)

1. carbohydrates	2. grain
3. bran	4. germ
5. heart	6. wild

Fiber (pg. 12)

1. fiber	2. grains
3. food	4. diet
5. overeat	6. intestines
7. cancer	
8. fruits	9. discomfort
10. grams	11. oatmeal

Nutrient Knowledge (pg. 13)

Protein: builds muscle
    extra stored as fat
    fish is a source
    milk is a source
    maintains body tissue
Carbohydrates: source of energy
    provides fiber
    fruits and vegetables are sources
    may prevent colon cancer
Fats: saturated and unsaturated
    associated with strokes
    milk is a source
    source of energy
    fish is a source
    saturated in animal products
    unsaturated in vegetables

Salt and Sugar
Salt and a Healthy Lifestyle (pg. 14)

1. salt
2. spoiling
3. high
4. stroke
5. bologna
6. sodium
7. diet
8. 2,400

Sugar and a Healthy Lifestyle (pg. 15)

1. calories
2. jellies
3. sugar
4. diet
5. sugar
6. diabetes
7. calories
8. fat
9. reduced

Understanding Cholesterol, Triglycerides, Blood Pressure, and Diabetes
Cholesterol and Triglycerides (pg. 17)

1. fat
2. cholesterol
3. lipoproteins
4. deposits
5. blood
6. bad
7. good
8. liver
9. diet
10. fats
11. 150
12. heart
13. calories
14. overweight
15. Exercising
16. saturated
17. medication

Blood Pressure and a Healthy Lifestyle (pg. 18)

1. arteries
2. rest
3. two
4. systolic
5. diastolic
6. difficult
7. strokes
8. average
9. 120/80
10. 140/90

Diabetes and a Healthy Lifestyle (pg. 19)

Checklist answers will vary. Students may want to consult with the school nurse or a doctor if there is a concern.

Assessing What Has Been Learned
Assessment 1: Matching (pg. 22)

1. i
2. d
3. c
4. l
5. e
6. b
7. f
8. k
9. n
10. h
11. a
12. j
13. g
14. m

Assessment 2: Word Choice (pg. 23)

1. protein
2. carbohydrates
3. fiber
4. fat
5. diabetes
6. cholesterol
7. triglycerides
8. arteries
9. systolic
10. diastolic

Assessment 3: Crossword Puzzle (pg. 24–25)

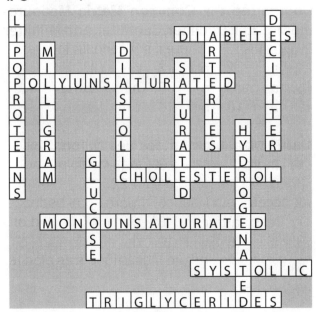

Daily Recommended Caloric Intake (pg. 26)
1. c   2. c   3. b   4. a
5. a

All You Can Eat (pg. 27)
Answers will vary, except:
3. calories

Diet Dilemma (pg. 29–30)
1. C; fruits   2. F; protein
3. E; milk   4. A; grains
5. B; vegetables   6. F; protein
7. E; milk   8. F; protein
9. B; vegetables   10. F; protein
11. D; milk   12. B; vegetables
13. C; fruits   14. F; protein
15. F; protein   16. B; vegetables
17. B; vegetables   18. A; grains
19. A; grains   20. C; fruits
Diet plans will vary.

Using Math to Understand Food Labels
Understanding Metric Measurement Prefixes (pg. 31)
1. b   2. a   3. c   4. b
5. a   6. c   7. b   8. a
9. c

Comparing the Common Metric Measurements Liter, Deciliter, Centiliter, and Milliliter (pg. 31)
1. a   2. b   3. c   4. c
5. a   6. c   7. a   8. a
9. b   10. b   11. c   12. c

Metric Measurement for Health (pg. 32)
1. more   2. 2.114
3. 3.171   4. 4.228
5. more   6. more
7. less, larger   8. c
9. c   10. d

Comparing Grams and Kilograms to Ounces and Pounds (pg. 33)
1. b   2. a   3. c   4. b
5. a   6. c   7. b   8. d
9. c   10. b   11. d   12. c
13. d   14. b

Assessment 4: Metric Measurements of Mass (pg. 34)
1. mg = milligram   kg = kilogram
   g = gram
2. gram; kilogram
3. 2.2   4. 28
5. 227
6. Ounces: 5   8   11   14
   Grams: 141.75 226.8 311.85   396.9
7. Kilograms: 1; 2; 3; 4; 5; 6; 7; 8; 9; 10

Understanding Percentages (pg. 35)
1. a.   200   b.   300
   c.   400   d.   500
   e.   278   f.   308
   g.   467   h.   45
   i.   4   j.   0.68
2. a, d, and e are greater than 1%.

Finding the Percentage (pg. 36)
1. 20   2. 17.5   3. 200
4. 500   5. 240   6. 45
7. 16.5   8. 25.5   9. 268
10. 5.52

Food Labels
Understanding Food Labels (pg. 37)
1. grams   2. milligrams
3. 3.6   4. 18   5. 2   6. 8

Finding Your Daily Requirement (pg. 38)
1. b   2. d

Food Label Practice (pg. 39)
1. 60   2. 15   3. 1.3
4. 1   5. 0   6. 5
7. 432   8. 19   9. 20
10. 300   11. 65

Analyzing Food Labels (pg. 40–41)
1. c 2. a 3. b 4. d
5. c 6. d 7. d 8. b
9. c 10. a

Comparing Food Labels (pg. 42–45)
1. c 2. c 3. a 4. a
5. c 6. d 7. a

Bread: 270; 3 g; 0 g; 0 mg; 510 mg; 51 g; 6 g

Cookies: 510; 24 g; 13.5 g; 0 mg; 165 mg; 57 g; 1.5 g

Cheese: 260; 22 g; 12 g; 60 mg; 400 mg; 2 g; 0 g

Granola Bars: 200; 13 g; 4 g; 0 mg; 160 mg; 42 g; 22 g

Total: 1,240; 62 g; 29.5 g; 60 mg; 1,235 mg; 152 g; 29.5 g

8. saturated fat
9. clogged
10. carbohydrates

Snacks from pg. 43: 1,240; 62 g; 29.5 g; 60 mg; 1,235 mg; 152 g; 29.5 g

Burger with cheese: 300; 12 g; 6 g; 40 mg; 750 mg; 33 g; 2 g

French fries: 500; 25 g; 3.5 g; 0 mg; 350 mg; 63 g; 6 g

Total: 2,040; 99 g; 39 g; 100 mg; 2,335 mg; 248 g; 37.5 g

11. a 12. fat 13. a 14. a
15. b 16. c 17. high blood
18. carbohydrates

Snacks from pg. 43: 1,240; 62 g; 29.5 g; 60 mg; 1,235 mg; 152 g; 29.5 g

Burger (no cheese): 250; 9 g; 3.5 g; 25 mg; 520 mg; 31 g; 2 g

Salad (with chicken): 220; 6 g; 3 g; 75 mg; 890 mg; 12 g; 3 g

Total: 1,710; 77 g; 36 g; 160 mg; 2,645 mg; 195 g; 34.5 g

19. T 20. T 21. T 22. T
23. T 24. F 25. T 26. T
27. T 28. T

Evaluating My Lifestyle
Figuring Body Mass Index (pg. 46)
1. BMI = 29 overweight
2. BMI = 39 obese
3. BMI = 24 normal
4. Answers will vary.

Profile for Better Health (pg. 47–48)
Profiles will vary.

Shape Up! (pg. 49–50)
1. calories, heart, lungs, blood, exercise, exercise, 200
2. tone, appearance, stress
3. exercise, routine, three, 20, shoes, water
4. fat, 35, overweight, blood pressure, cancer
5. fruits, vegetables, fiber, cancer, intestinal
6. Vitamins, carrots, sweet potatoes, oranges, grapefruit

Diet and Exercise: Persuasive Letter (pg. 51)
Letters will vary.

Nutritional Choices: Face the Consequences (pg. 52)
1. Short-term consequences: overweight, loss of energy, poor self-concept
Long-term consequences: fatty buildup, loss of lifestyle, overweight, atherosclerosis
Ultimate consequences: heart attack, stroke/life threatened
2. Short-term consequences: more energy, better self-concept, better physical appearance
Long-term consequences: improved health, lower cholesterol level, atherosclerosis less likely, less chance for heart attack
Ultimate consequences: lower medical expenses, longer life, more productive life

Eating Disorders: Anorexia and Bulimia (pg. 53)
Answers will vary. Consult the school nurse or a doctor if there is a concern.

Nutrition Review Cloze (pg. 54–59)

1. muscle	2. growth		
3. fat	4. weight		
5. proteins	6. beans		
7. meat	8. protein		
9. ounces	10. cholesterol		
11. carbohydrates	12. grain		
13. bran	14. germ		
15. heart	16. wild		
17. fiber	18. food		
19. diet	20. overeat		
21. cancer	22. vegetables		
23. fruits	24. fiber		
25. diet	26. energy		
27. diabetes	28. animal		
29. room	30. cholesterol		
31. blood	32. fat		
33. saturated	34. cholesterol		
35. limited	36. polyunsaturated		
37. plant	38. omega-3		
39. cholesterol	40. trans		
41. cookies	42. limited		
43. calories	44. jellies		
45. diet	46. weight		
47. sugar	48. calories		
49. diabetes	50. fat		
51. reduced	52. spoiling		
53. salt	54. high		
55. stroke	56. bologna		
57. diet	58. vegetables		
59. sugar	60. calories		
61. healthy	62. diseases		
63. weight	64. exercise		
65. physical	66. energy		
67. diseases	68. blood		
69. cholesterol	70. arteries		
71. blood	72. heart		
73. diastolic	74. stroke		
75. fat	76. cholesterol		
77. deposits	78. blood		
79. good	80. diet		
81. adults	82. diabetes		
83. glucose	84. bruises		

Living With Stress De-Stressing (pg. 63)
1. B, H 2. F, H 3. B, H 4. E
5. C, E 6. A, E 7. D 8. G

Learning About HIV, AIDS, and Sexually Transmitted Diseases
HIV and AIDS: A Fact of Life (pg. 68–69)

1. immune	2. viruses
3. white	4. immune
5. white	6. antibodies
7. T/B	8. B/T
9. killer	10. B
11. antibodies	12. antibodies
13. virus	14. memory
15. virus	16. antibodies
17. slowly	18. many
19. HIV	20. cocktail

21. bleeding gums or nose
22. fevers of 100 for ten days or more
23. night sweats
24. weight loss
25. diarrhea
26. swollen lymph nodes
27. headache
28. sores or white spots in the mouth
29. memory problems
30. A, B, C, D, F

HIV and AIDS: Crossword Puzzle (pg. 70)

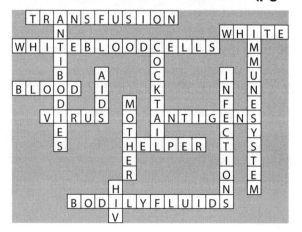

HIV and AIDS: Fact or Fiction? (pg. 71)

2. sexual intercourse,
   sharing a syringe or needle,
   to unborn child during mother's pregnancy,
   blood transfusion (very unlikely today)
3. all except the answers from #2

Sexually Transmitted Diseases (pg. 73)

Plus signs should be placed on 1, 3, 6, 7, 9.

Learning About Drugs
Oh, What a Tangled Web (pg. 77)

Teacher check that web is filled out with reasonable answers.

Drug Use: Face the Consequences (pg. 78)

Answers may vary. Accept all reasonable consequences.
1. Immediate consequences: mental confusion, bizarre behavior, severe motor problems, increased blood pressure, increased body temperature, increased heart rate, aggression, death
   Health consequences: HIV infection, insomnia, loss of appetite, miscarriage, emphysema, withdrawal, death
   Legal consequences: arrest, court supervision

Drug Use: Crossword Puzzle (pg. 79)

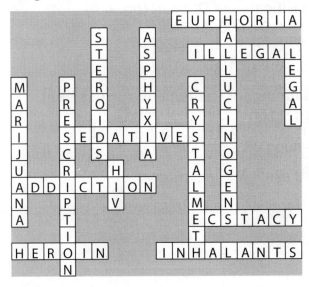

Learning About Tobacco
And I'll Huff and I'll Puff . . . (pg. 82)

Positive Tobacco Images:
   people enjoying outdoor activities, people having fun, healthy people, people who are clean and neatly dressed, people laughing, people smiling and happy, people who look physically strong, young, enjoy life, attractive

Negative Tobacco Images:
   people told they have bad breath, discolored teeth, unhealthy lungs, inhale and cough, clothes smell, wrinkled skin, sick babies, discussing nicotine

To Smoke or Not to Smoke (pg. 84)

1. Nicotine is habit forming.
2. to make the taste more appealing
3. $56; $240; $2,920; $116,800
4. Answers will vary.
5. T   6. F   7. T   8. F

Learning About Alcohol
Exploring Alcohol Myths (pg. 85)

1. -	2. +	3. -	4. -
5. +	6. -	7. +	8. +
9. -	10. -	11. -	12. -
13. +	14. -	15. +	16. +
17. +	18. +	19. +	20. +
21. -	22. +	23. -	24. -
25. +	26. +	27. +	28. -
29. +	30. +		

Medical studies vary on #14 and #21.

Think Before You Drink (pg. 87)

1. 20 proof; 80 calories
2. 10 proof; 96 calories
3. 40 percent; 96 calories
4. fermentation   5. inhibition
6. alcohol   7. proof
8. intoxicated   9. depressant
10. sedative   11. tranquilizer
12. alcoholic

It's Up to You: Fetal Alcohol Syndrome (pg. 88)

1. answers like not blaming, not arguing, having accurate information, no threats to withhold love
2. accurate and factual information from health experts and doctors
3. doing something with you that you both enjoy, having other friends in who will not encourage the family member to drink
4. do not give your approval; indicate you are concerned and want the best for the family member; offer to be available if needed; leave the situation with the family member realizing your concerns but your love for them, too

Blood Alcohol Content: Its Effect on You (pg. 91)

1. the weight of drinker; the amount of alcohol consumed
2. A   3. 3   4. 9   5. $1\frac{1}{2}$ 6. 6

Exploring Stereotypes
American Melting Pot (pg. 98)

1. G   2. F   3. I   4. E
5. B   6. C   7. H   8. D
9. -   10. +   11. +   12. -
13. -   14. -   15. -   16. -
17. -   18. -   19. -   20. +
21. -   22. -   23. -   24. -
25. +

Financial Health
Paying for a Loan (pg. 106–107)

Total interest: $32.80
1. a.   Avg.: $300   Interest: $15
   b.   Avg.: $900   Interest: $54
   c.   Avg.: $1,200   Interest: $96
2. a.   Avg.: $900   Interest: $67.50
   b.   Avg.: $900   Interest: $108
   c.   Avg.: $1,200   Interest: $252
   d.   Avg.: $1,500   Interest: $360

Car Depreciation (pg. 108)

1. Interest per month: $10
   Amt. paid: $9,840   Amt. owed: $14,760
   Difference: $2,760   Still owe: $2,760

2. Interest per month: $12.50
   Amt. paid: $12,300   Amt. owed: $12,300
   Difference: $300   Still owe: $300

Computing Car Costs (pg. 109)

Answers will vary according to state and city tax rates, price of insurance and license, etc.

Figuring the Cost for Gas (pg. 110)

1. c   2. a   3. b
4. b   5. d   6. b
7. a   8. c   9. d

Planning for Retirement
Social Security Trust Fund (pg. 111–112)

1. a. $24.80   b. $5.80   c. $30.60
2. a. $31 + $7.25 = $38.25
   b. $31 + $7.25 = $38.25
   c. $62 + $14.50 = $76.50
3. a. $62   b. $14.50   c. $76.50
   d. $423.50

Retirement Age (pg. 113)

1. Answers will vary.
2. 2024   3. 2045   4. 2022

Savings Accounts: Simple Interest (pg. 114)

1. 0.04 x $2,000 = $80   2. $2,080
3. 0.03 x $3,000 = $90   4. $3,090
5. 0.04 x $2,500 = $100   6. $2,600

Compound Interest (pg. 115)

1. b   2. d

Certificates of Deposit (pg. 116)

1. 0.04; $40; $1,040
2. 0.06; $120; $2,120
3. 0.05; $150; $3,150

Planning for Retirement: Assessment (pg. 117)

1. b   2. b   3. d   4. b
5. d   6. c   7. c   8. $2,080
9. c   10. a